ESSENTIALS OF BASIC PROGRAMMING

THE IRWIN SERIES IN INFORMATION AND DECISION SCIENCES

Consulting Editors Robert B. Fetter, *Yale University*; Claude McMillan, *University of Colorado*

ESSENTIALS OF BASIC PROGRAMMING

RALPH M. STAIR, JR.
The Florida State University

RALPH E. JANARO
Clarkson College of Technology

1981

RICHARD D. IRWIN, INC. HOMEWOOD, ILLINOIS 60430

ISBN 0-256-02389-1
Library of Congress Catalog Card No. 80-82452
Printed in the United States of America

7 8 9 0 K 8 7 6 5 4 3

TO LILA AND HELEN

Preface

The purpose of this text is to present the fundamentals of BASIC programming. Although this text is small and inexpensive, it covers major statements that can be found in books costing twice as much. This book has been designed to be used as a supplement to *Principles of Data Processing* by Stair. It can also be used with other books on computers and data processing or by itself for a course in BASIC programming.

The material has been organized into chapters that flow logically from one topic to the next. Before any new statement is introduced, students are shown why the statement is important and the types of problems that the statement can solve. This is followed by a clear explanation of the statement and one or more examples. In addition, each chapter contains several applications that reveal how a particular statement or a group of statements can be used to solve useful and realistic problems. Each chapter contains a number of questions. Each question has been designed to test a student's understanding of a particular statement or concept.

We would like to thank Claude McMillan and Robert Fetter for their comments and suggestions. In addition, we would like to acknowledge the support of Bill Anthony, the Department of Management, and the College of Business at Florida State University.

RMS
REJ

Contents

1. Introduction to program and application development 1

Preprogramming activities (planning). Requirements: *Requirements for Sound System, Inc.* Analysis: *Analysis for Sound System, Inc.* Programming: *The program for Sound System, Inc.* Postprogramming activities. Testing: *Program testing for Sound System, Inc. Implementation.*

2. Introduction to BASIC 13

Advantages of BASIC: *Application 2-1. Application 2-2. Application 2-3. Application 2-4.* Writing computer programs: *Learning how to write BASIC programs. About making mistakes. Spaces within a line.* Correcting and running your program using a terminal.

3. Fundamental concepts in BASIC 21

Numbers. E notation. Variables. Predefined functions. Expressions. BASIC statements and line numbers. REM.

4. Writing simple programs with END, PRINT, and LET 29

END. PRINT: *Application 4-1. Application 4-2. Application 4-3.* LET: *Application 4-4.* A possible error: Undefined variables: *Application 4-5. A. Desired output. B. Required data. C. Program.*

5. Writing realistic and useful programs with READ, INPUT, GO TO, IF, and ON–GO TO 45

READ and DATA statements: *Application 5-1.* INPUT: *Application 5-2.* GO TO: *Application 5-3. Application 5-4.* IF: *Application 5-5.* ON–GO TO: *Application 5-6.*

6. Gateway to effective and efficient programming with FOR—NEXT and subscripted variables **59**

FOR and NEXT: *Application 6-1. Application 6-2. Application 6-3. Application 6-4.* RESTORE: *Application 6-5.* Subscripted variables. Dimension: *Application 6-6. Application 6-7.*

7. Some additional features of BASIC including string variables, PRINT USING, TAB, and RND **79**

String variables and constants: *Application 7-1.* PRINT USING: *Application 7-2.* TAB: *Application 7-3.* Random numbers: *Application 7-4.*

8. Using subroutines and user-defined functions with DEF and GO SUB **91**

DEF: *Application 8-1.* GO SUB—RETURN: *Application 8-2.*

9. Matrix operations with MAT, READ, INPUT, PRINT, TRN, INV, IDN, and more **97**

MAT statements: *Application 9-1. Application 9-2. Application 9-3.* CON, ZER, IDN, TRN, and INV: *Application 9-4. Application 9-5.*

10. Data files with FILES, SCRATCH, RESTORE, READ, WRITE, and IF **107**

Creating data files: *Application 10-1.* The use of data files: *Application 10-3. Application 10-4.*

Index **115**

1 Introduction to program and application development

All of our lives have been altered as a result of the increased use of computer systems. Your checking account, phone bill, magazine subscriptions, and student records are examples. Unfortunately, at one time or another most of us have been victims of mistakes that occasionally occur in computer systems. It is unknown how many millions of dollars have been lost through these errors by companies of all sizes as well as governmental and nonprofit agencies at all levels, but the amount is large. You may be saying to yourself, "That cursed computer did it again," but these problems are not normally the fault of the computer equipment. You would not blame a hammer for a poorly driven nail, or a mixing bowl for a cake that had a horrible taste, and you should not blame the computer because you received the wrong phone bill or no magazine this month. Like the hammer or the mixing bowl, the computer is a tool, a tool we use to help us process data. The success or failure of a computer system to produce meaningful results does not, in general, depend on the computer equipment. It depends on the success or failure of people to use this electronic tool properly.

A computer program is the means by which people can control the computer to produce meaningful and beneficial output, but writing successful computer programs is not an easy task. How to write successful programs will be outlined in this chapter. To begin, we will look into what should be done before a program is written.

PREPROGRAMMING ACTIVITIES (PLANNING)

Some programming books lead you to believe that very little or nothing has to be done before introducing a program into a computer system; you just write the program on the back of an envelope or on a scrap piece of paper and then run it on the computer. Doing this for a program of any size would be like sketching a house on a soiled place mat or napkin at a restaurant, and then beginning to construct the house without any blueprints or detailed plans. In both cases, the chances of success are small indeed.

REQUIREMENTS

Computer programs are written because there is a problem to be solved or a need to be satisfied. Perhaps a medical clinic needs tighter controls on unpaid bills, or the police department has a problem in obtaining a fast and complete list of possible suspects for a crime, given partial descriptions such as a scar, foreign accent, nervous twitch in the left eye, hair color, height, and so on. Once the problem or need has been identified, the reports or information desired from the computer system, *output requirements,* and the data needed to produce these reports, *input requirements,* should be completely specified.

Requirements for Sound System, Inc.

The general manager of Sound System, Inc., a producer of tweeters, midranges, woofers, horns, crossover systems, and other speaker parts, is concerned with rising payroll costs. After discussing the problem with the data processing department, the manager decided that a report should be prepared by the computer at 8:30 a.m. every Tuesday. The report should list all employees whose gross pay ex-

FIGURE 1-1
Output requirements

EXCEPTION REPORT
Prepared for B. Render, General Manager

Employee No.	Hours	Rate	Gross
1222	60	7	420
1225	50	10.10	505
.			
.			
.			

The supervisors for the above employees should be consulted.

ceeded $400 for the previous week. To detail these needs to the data processing department, the general manager has drawn up a sample of the report that is to be generated by the computer system. It appears in Figure 1-1.

Now that the output has been specified, what input data is needed, and where is the data stored? Usually the data will be stored on disk, tape, or computer cards. We will assume that the data is already on computer cards from another program that prints the weekly pay checks; the last data card contains three zeros separated with commas to signify that there is no more data. Sample data appears in Table 1-1.

TABLE 1-1
Input requirements

Required data			*Employee number*	*Hours*	*Rate*
Variables to be used →			*N*	*H*	*R*
Sample DATA statements →	1000	DATA	1222,	60,	7
	1001	DATA	1223,	40,	5
	1002	DATA	1225,	50,	10.10
	.				
	.				
	.				
	9000	DATA	0,	0,	0

ANALYSIS

Once the output and input requirements have been determined, the next step is to develop detailed plans that will be used in writing the program. Like a blueprint for a house, flowcharts are used in specifying how the computer program is to be written or constructed. This analysis also reveals how the input data is to be processed to get the desired reports.

Analysis for Sound System, Inc.

The first step is to develop a flowchart for the application. Some of the symbols used in application flowcharting are on page 4. A complete set of symbols used in application and program flowcharting can be drawn with the aid of the template shown in Figure 1-2.

The purpose of an application flowchart is to use symbols to give

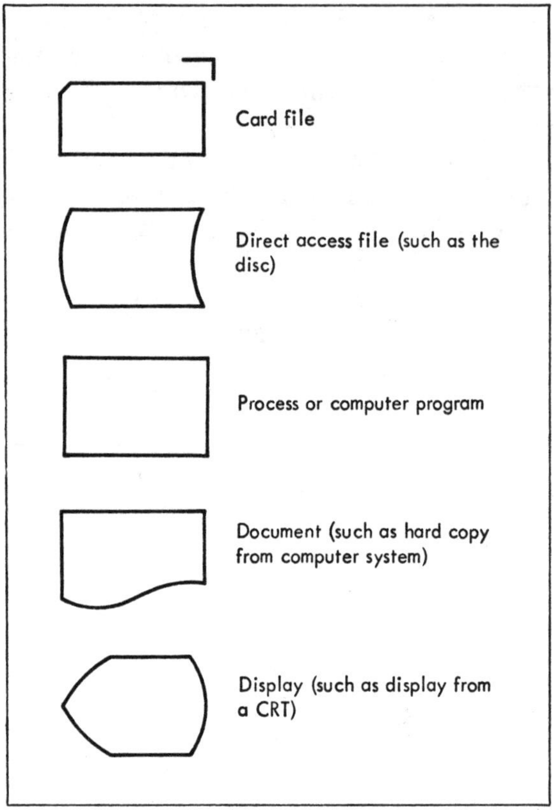

FIGURE 1-2
Template for drawing symbols used in application and program flowcharting

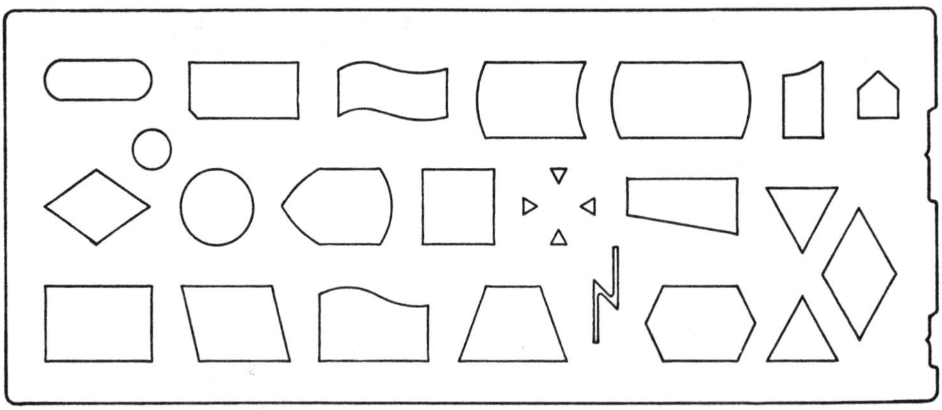

Source: This material is reproduced with permission from American National Standard X3.5–1970. © 1970 by the American National Standards Institute. Copies may be purchased from the American National Standards Institute, 1430 Broadway, New York.

a general picture of what functions the computer system should perform. The application flowchart reveals how many programs are to be written, what reports or documents are to be produced, and the form and source of the input data.

The application flowchart for Sound System, Inc., is straightforward. The program should read data from a card file and print a document containing a list of all employees earning over $400 per week. See Figure 1-3.

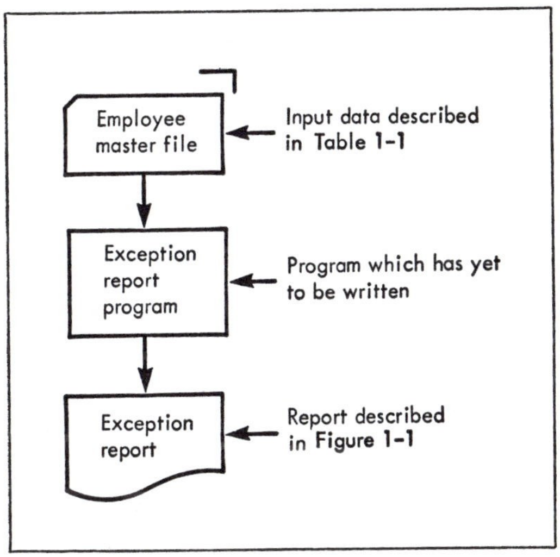

FIGURE 1-3
Application flowchart for Sound System, Inc.

The application flowchart in Figure 1-3 gives an overall picture of the application. But how should the program be designed and written? We must analyze the exception report program in more detail. Like the application flowchart, the program flowchart uses symbols to describe computer actions. Some of these symbols are on page 6.

Now, the next step is to use these symbols to construct a program flowchart. But how is this done? One approach is to think about how you would generate the exception report by hand, using pencil and paper. Here is what you might do:

1. Start the analysis.
2. Print the headings for the exception report.
3. Read N, H, R (the employee number, hours worked, and rate).
4. Is N = 0? (When N is 0, there is no more data.)
   a. No—go to the next statement, which is number 5.
   b. Yes—go to statement 8, which prints the final message.
5. Let G be equal to H times R. This calculates the gross pay.

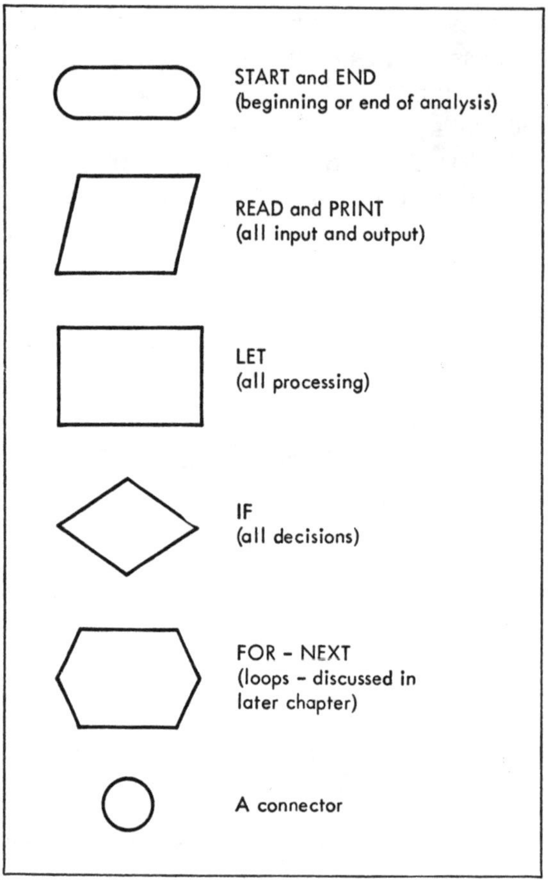

6. Is G less than or equal to $400 for this employee?
   a. Yes–go to statement 3 and process another employee.
   b. No–go to the next statement, which is number 7.
7. Print N, H, R, G. (Print the employee number, hours, rate, and gross pay.) Then go to statement 3 and process another employee.
8. Print the final message, which is "THE SUPERVISORS FOR THE ABOVE EMPLOYEES SHOULD BE CONSULTED."
9. End the analysis.

You may have done this in a different manner, but the results would have been the same. Now, we will develop the program flowchart. For your convenience, the above numbers have been included (see Figure 1-4).

The flowchart in Figure 1-4 graphically displays the same information as described above. After the headings such as "EXCEPTION REPORT" are printed, N, H, and R are READ. If N = 0, then there

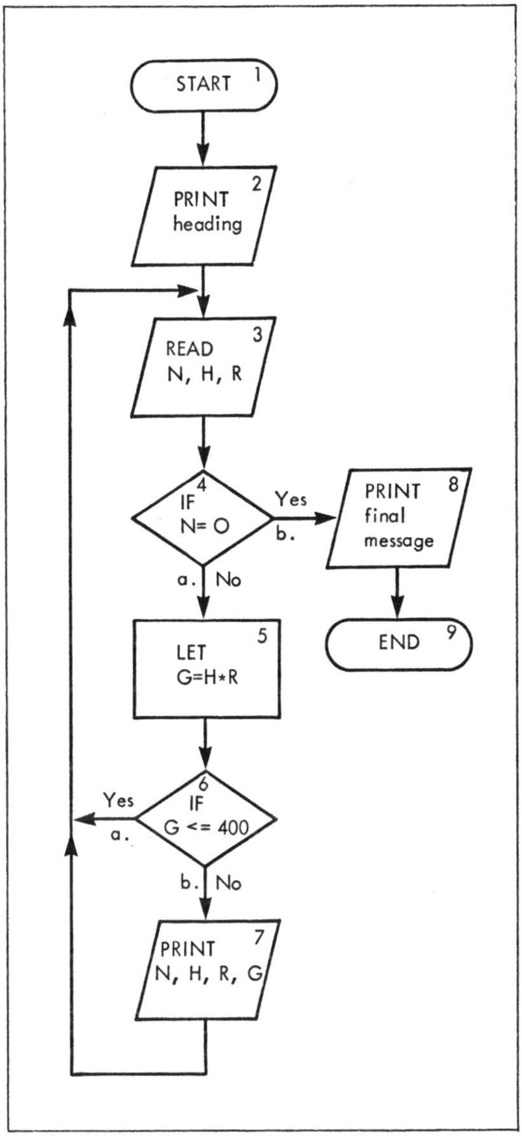

FIGURE 1-4
Flowchart for Sound System, Inc.

is no more data, and the program stops after printing a brief message. Otherwise gross pay, G, is calculated, and checked to see if it is greater than 400. If G is greater than 400, N, H, R, and G are printed as requested by the general manager, after which the program instructs the computer to loop back and process the data for the next employee. Of course, if G is not greater than 400, the program instructs the computer to loop back to process the data for the next employee without any printing.

PROGRAMMING

Writing the program is the next step. Because this will be the subject of the following chapters, a detailed discussion will not be given here. It should be mentioned, however, that the program should be as simple and as straightforward as possible. This will make modifying the program later, if it is needed, easier and less confusing.

The program for Sound System, Inc.

Using all the documents developed in the preprogramming steps, a programmer in the data processing department was able to write the necessary program. The program is shown below:

Program 1-1

```
10 PRINT "EXCEPTION REPORT"
20 PRINT "PREPARED FOR B. RENDER, GENERAL MANAGER"
30 PRINT
40 PRINT "EMPLOYEE NO.","HOURS","RATE","GROSS"
50 READ N,H,R
60 IF N = 0, GO TO 110
70 LET G = H * R
80 IF G< = 400, GO TO 50
90 PRINT N,H,R,G
100 GO TO 10
110 PRINT "THE SUPERVISOR FOR THE ABOVE"
120 PRINT "EMPLOYEES SHOULD BE CONSULTED"
1000 DATA 1222,60,7
1001 DATA 1223,40,5
1002 DATA 1225,50,10.10
9000 DATA 0,0,0
9999 END
```

It must be stressed that you are not expected to understand the above program. It is only given here to show the natural progression of developing a successful computer program. As you look at the instructions in the program, however, you should note the similarity between it and the program flowchart previously given.

POSTPROGRAMMING ACTIVITIES

Many mishaps and computer system errors are caused by not completely performing postprogramming activities. The following activities are easy to perform, and they can prevent untold problems.

TESTING

Every statement must be tested to assure that there are no programming mistakes (called "bugs"). Test data must be developed that will test every part of the program. If this is not done, a mistake in a program may go undetected for months. You may hear someone from the data processing department screaming with panic, "The program developed a 'bug' today."

Of course, the program mistake didn't magically develop in the program after it was written. The mistake was always in the program, but the part of the program containing the mistake may not have been executed for a long time. Thus it is important to develop test data that will test *every* statement in the program.

Program testing for Sound System, Inc.

The following output was obtained from the program.

```
? INITIAL PART OF STATEMENT NEITHER MATCHES A STATEMENT KEYWORD NOR HAS
A FORM THAT IS LEGAL--CHECK MISSPELLING IN LINE 110
```

Output from Program 1-1

As seen from the output, some type of mistake has been made in line 110. Look at line 110 in Program 1-1. The keyword "PRINT" has been misspelled. This type of error is a grammatical mistake, which results in an error message. When line 110 is retyped and the mistake corrected, the program gives the following output from the computer.

```
READY
RUNNH


EXCEPTION REPORT
PREPARED FOR B. RENDER, GENERAL MANAGER

EMPLOYEE NO.  HOURS          RATE          GROSS
 1222          60             7             420
EXCEPTION REPORT
PREPARED FOR B. RENDER, GENERAL MANAGER

EMPLOYEE NO.  HOURS          RATE          GROSS
 1225          50             10.1          505.
EXCEPTION REPORT
PREPARED FOR B. RENDER, GENERAL MANAGER

EMPLOYEE NO.  HOURS          RATE          GROSS
THE SUPERVISOR FOR THE ABOVE
EMPLOYEES SHOULD BE CONSULTED
```

Output from Program 1-1

As you can see, there is still something wrong with the computer program. The headings should be printed only once. Look at line 100 in the program, and compare it to the flowchart. Do you see the problem? Line 100 directs the computer to GO TO 10, where the headings are printed. Line 100 should be GO TO 50 to process another employee. When this correction is made, the program will work. See Program 1-2.

Program 1-2

```
10 PRINT "EXCEPTION REPORT"
20 PRINT "PREPARED FOR B. RENDER, GENERAL MANAGER"
30 PRINT
40 PRINT "EMPLOYEE NO.","HOURS","RATE","GROSS"
50 READ N,H,R
60 IF N = 0, GO TO 110
70 LET G = H * R
80 IF G< = 400, GO TO 50
90 PRINT N,H,R,G
100 GO TO 50
110 PRINT "THE SUPERVISOR FOR THE ABOVE"
120 PRINT "EMPLOYEES SHOULD BE CONSULTED"
1000 DATA 1222,60,7
1001 DATA 1223,40,5
1002 DATA 1225,50,10.10
9000 DATA 0,0,0
9999 END

READY
RUNNH


EXCEPTION REPORT
PREPARED FOR B. RENDER, GENERAL MANAGER

EMPLOYEE NO.  HOURS          RATE           GROSS
 1222          60             7              420
 1225          50             10.1           505.
THE SUPERVISOR FOR THE ABOVE
EMPLOYEES SHOULD BE CONSULTED
```

Reflect a moment. If the test data did not include an employee whose gross pay exceeded $400, this error would not have been detected because the statement in line 80 would always send the computer to line 50, and statements below line 80 would not have been tested. Thus it is important to prepare test data that tests *every* statement in the program.

Implementation

The final step is to *phase in* the use of this program to produce the exception report that is to be presented to the general manager every Tuesday morning. If this report is now being produced manually, then both the manual report and the computer-prepared report should be run together in *parallel* until everyone is confident that the computer is preparing the report as expected. Then the manual report may be *phased out;* the new computer program is now running smoothly and providing the desired information to the general manager.

SUMMARY

Great speeches have been scribbled on the back of envelopes, but, in general, successful computer programs require more planning. Steps in writing a program are like links in a chain. If one is weak or absent, there will be trouble. In computer programming, what *can* go wrong *will* go wrong. In this chapter, the minimum requirements for building a successful computer program have been outlined.

You may have been wondering what should be done when several programs interact, and the output from one becomes the input to another. The procedures outlined in this chapter should be logically expanded to analyze the entire system of programs. Starting with definition of output requirements and ending with implementation, the entire system of programs should be considered in addition to each individual program in the system. The procedures outlined do not substantially change when more complex applications are developed.

Sound System, Inc. summary

To bring meaning and realism to the procedures mentioned in this chapter, an application for Sound System, Inc., was examined. It was assumed that the data was on computer cards and that this data was used with a different program to produce weekly paychecks. Of course, the data could be on disk or magnetic tape, and the program discussed in this chapter may be one of several programs that comprise a system of programs that write the checks and produce quarterly reports, W-2 forms, and other reports.

It should also be mentioned that special forms exist to help in specifying output and input requirements, developing flowcharts, and writing computer programs.

QUESTIONS

1-1. What is the cause of most computer-related mistakes and problems?

1-2. What is involved in determining output requirements?

1-3. What is the purpose of testing? How should it be accomplished?

Introduction to BASIC

2

ADVANTAGES OF BASIC

One reason that BASIC is so popular is its conversational nature. A BASIC program is very similar to the instructions you would write for a person. BASIC makes communicating with a computer natural, simple, and straightforward.

Another advantage of BASIC is its many built-in conveniences. Handling a large table of numbers can be very difficult in other programming languages. In BASIC you can command the computer to print a table of more than 100 numbers or names with one simple instruction.

To get you started, here are some BASIC computer programs. Do not try to understand the details. Relax and try to get the flavor of programming.

Application 2-1

BASIC can be used like a hand calculator. If you want to find the circumference of a circle with a diameter of four inches, you multiply 4 times a constant π, which is 3.14159. The following BASIC program will make this calculation:

Program 2-1

```
10 LET C=4*3.14159
20 PRINT C
30 END
RUNNH

 12.5664
```

This is the program that you type. (points to lines 10–30)

RUNNH means run with no heading. You type this. (points to RUNNH)

This is the output from the computer. It is printed after you type RUNNH and hit the return key. (points to 12.5664)

Application 2-2

You can also instruct the computer to read data and make computations before the results are printed. Here is a program that will calculate a 15 percent commission, C, on sales, S.

Program 2-2

Program →

```
10 READ S
20 LET C = .15*S
30 PRINT C
40 DATA 400
50 END

RUNNH
 60
```

The program is run. (→ RUNNH)

Here is the output

This program reads the sales amount $400 from the DATA statement, calculates the commission in line 20, and prints the commission in line 30.

Figure 2-1 is the flowchart for Program 2-2.

FIGURE 2-1
Flowchart for application 2-2

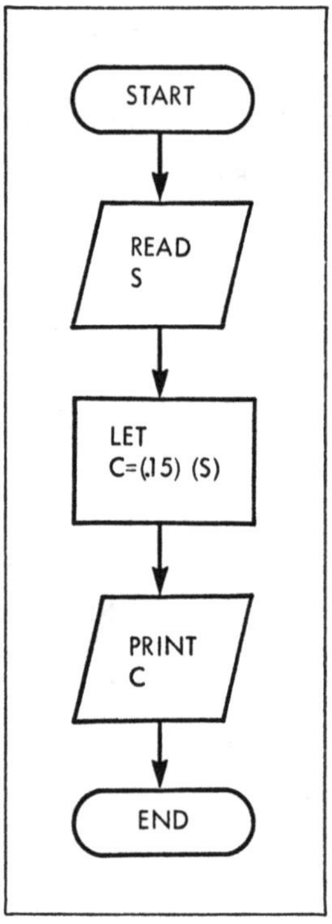

Application 2-3

How could you modify the above program to calculate the commission for each sale during the month? Assume you make the following sales in dollars: 400, 100, 2,000, 500, 1,062.47, and 342.61. Of course, you could write the above program six times to calculate the commission on the six sales, but there is a much easier way, as seen in Program 2-3.

Program 2-3

```
10 READ S
20 LET C = .15*S
30 PRINT C
35 GO TO 10
40 DATA 400,100,2000,500,1062.47,342.61
50 END

RUNNH


 60
 15
 300
 75
 159.371
 51.3915
```

The only change is a GO TO 10 statement in line 35 that instructs the computer to read the next sales value from the data statement, after which the computer continues as usual.

As can be seen, this program creates a *loop* that cycles once for each value in the DATA statement. If we had 100 sales amounts in several DATA statements, this program would loop 100 times, calculating and printing the commission for each sale.

After all the data is read, there will be an "out-of data" error message. You will learn how to avoid this in Chapter 5.

Application 2-4

Assume that the sales manager decided to offer a $100 bonus above the normal 15 percent commission for any sale that is $1,000 or more. This new bonus offer can be incorporated into the above program as shown in Program 2-4.

All we have done is add two new lines to get Program 2-4. Here is how the program works. The first sales value to be processed is 400. This value is read in line 10 and the commission is computed in line 20 as usual. Since 400 is less than 1,000, line 24 directs the computer to go directly to line 30. The commission is printed, and then

Program 2-4

```
10 READ S
20 LET C = .15*S
24 IF S<1000 THEN 30
26 LET C = C + 100
30 PRINT C
35 GO TO 10
40 DATA 400,100,2000,500,1062.47,342.61
50 END

READY
RUNNH


 60
 15
 400
 75
 259.371
 51.3915
```

line 35 sends us back to line 10 for the second loop, which is processed the same as the first loop. The third loop, where S is set equal to 2,000 in line 10, is different. When we get to line 24, since 2,000 is *not* less than 1,000, the computer drops down to line 26 and adds $100 to the commission. Thus, whenever S is 1,000 or greater, 100 is added to C.

WRITING COMPUTER PROGRAMS

The rest of this book will provide the ammunition you need to write efficient and effective computer programs. Soon you will be giving decisive commands to the computer such as these–READ X,Y,Z–LET A = (X + Y + Z)/3–GO TO 10. The purpose of any BASIC programming book is to teach you how to control or command the computer using a new language called BASIC.

Learning how to write BASIC programs

Learning BASIC is like learning to speak a foreign language, with one exception: BASIC is infinitely easier to learn. Whereas the average pocket dictionary contains about 50,000 words, there are fewer than 50 commands in BASIC. Indeed, you could learn all the commands in less than a day. A collection of *all* BASIC commands would occupy less than two typed pages.

It usually takes longer than one day, however, to become a proficient programmer in the BASIC language. As with any language, knowing only the grammar or mechanics of the language is not enough. You must also know how to construct or use a collection of commands to force the computer system to generate the results you desire. This challenge can be fun, though on occasion, it can be very frustrating. As you progress through this book, make a special note of how each command is used to bring about a desired result from the computer system.

About making mistakes

Regardless of the care you take in writing computer programs, you will make mistakes. But it is refreshing to know that there are only two types of mistakes you can make. A knowledge of these types will help in early detection and correction.

A *grammatical* error will result in an error message:

```
10  LET A = (10 + 8)/2
20  PRIMT "THE AVERAGE OF 10 AND 8 IS"; A
30  END
```

When line 20 is changed and the word PRINT is correctly spelled, the above program runs without any problems.

A *logical* error will not result in an error message, but the computer will produce output that is not correct.

```
10  LET A = 10 + 8/2
20  PRINT "THE AVERAGE OF 10 AND 8 IS"; A
30  END
```

The computer will compute and print:

```
THE AVERAGE OF 10 AND 8 IS 14
```

The computer divided 8 by 2 and then added 10 to the result to get 14. Parentheses around the 10 and 8 are needed to rid this program of the error.

If you get an error message, check for a grammatical mistake such as spelling. If you get the wrong output, check your logic in the program.

Spaces within a line

The computer ignores all spaces except those within quotation marks. Thus you should put spaces within a line to make the line easy for you and others to read and understand.

CORRECTING AND RUNNING YOUR PROGRAM USING A TERMINAL

How do you run a BASIC program after you have written it? The procedure is straightforward, but it varies considerably from system to system. Thus we will only give you a few examples of how it might be done. Although your computer system will be somewhat different, you might be interested in seeing how you would start at the terminal and run a computer program. Every line that you would have to type has been underlined. The return key must be hit after every line that you type. The examples are below.

Example 1

. LOG	You type "LOG."
ID = 2306,306	You enter your computer number.
PASSWORD: RMS	You enter your password.
. R BASIC	This gets you into BASIC.
READY	The computer is READY for you to start.
NEW	You tell the computer that this is a new program.
NEW FILE NAME—ONE	You give a name to the program. It is "ONE."
READY	The computer is READY.
10 LET C = 4*3.14159	
20 PRINT C	You enter line 10 and 20 of Application 2-1.
30 ENT/T/D	You make a mistake in line 30 and correct it by hitting the rubout key.
LIST	You tell the computer to list your program.
10 LET C = 4*3.14159	Here is line 10.
20 PRINT C	Here is line 20.
30 END	Here is line 30 with the mistake removed.
READY	The computer is again READY.
RUN	You RUN your program.
12.5664	Here is the output from your program.
READY	The computer is READY for more.
MONITOR	This gets you back to the monitor level.
EXIT	The computer is leaving BASIC and going to the monitor level.
. KJ	You Kill the Job or get off the computer.
USER 2306,306 LOGGED OFF	The computer is ready for another person.

Example 2

HELLO-4110,RNS	This is your computer number and password.
ILLEGAL ACCESS	You made a mistake in the above line.
HELLO-4110-RMS	This time you enter the correct password.
ILLEGAL FORMAT	Something is wrong with the format.

HELLO-4110,RMS	You put a comma between 4110 and RMS.
READY	The computer is ready.
NAME-ONE	You name your program- "ONE."
READY	The computer is ready.
10 LET C = 4*3.14159	You enter line 10.
20 PRINR C	You enter line 20.
30 END	You enter line 30.
20 PRINT C	You see a mistake in line 20 and correct it.
LIST	You list your program.
10 LET C = 4*3.14159 20 PRINT C 30 END	Your program is listed by the computer.
READY	The computer is ready.
SAVE	You save your program so you can use it at another time.
RUN	You run the program.
12.5664	Here is the output.
BYE	You say good BYE to the computer.
0003 MINUTES OF TERMINAL TIME	Here is how long you were on the computer.

You might be tempted to try one of these examples. You will find that it will not work. You will need a computer number and a password assigned to you before the computer will allow you to run a program. Furthermore, your computer system will most likely require a slightly different procedure. This information will be given to you by your instructor or perhaps in a computer demonstration. As soon as you are given this information, you may want to try some of the programs in this chapter.

SUMMARY

Perhaps you were able to understand a couple of the example programs in this chapter. At this stage, it is important not to get overconfident because, even though some of these programs seem intuitive, following your intuition can be a mistake. Consider the following program that attempts to multiply 2,000 by 4.7:

```
10  LET C = 2,000*4.7
20  PRINT C
30  END
```

Your intuition may tell you that the above program will work. It is almost the same as Example Program 2-1, but the above program has an error in line 10. Can you tell what the error is? It is the comma in the number 2000. BASIC does not allow commas within a number. The following program will run without errors:

```
10 LET C = 2000*4.7
20 PRINT C
30 END
```

There are not many rules, but they must be followed exactly. If you do not learn the fundamentals now, you may experience many minor problems throughout the remainder of this book. When you have mastered the fundamental concepts, everything else is much easier. Since learning these fundamentals is so important, an entire chapter has been devoted to the subject. As you may have guessed, the next chapter is Fundamental Concepts in BASIC.

QUESTIONS

2-1. Discuss some of the advantages of BASIC.

2-2. What types of mistakes can you make in writing a BASIC program?

2-3. Describe how you would run a program on a teletype or terminal.

Fundamental concepts in BASIC

3

Writing computer programs is like building a house. Certain fundamental construction materials are required, and to do a good job you must know and be able to use these materials. Regardless of size or sophistication, a BASIC program is constructed from BASIC statements or instructions. You saw some sample BASIC statements in the last chapter. Any BASIC statement can be constructed from *numbers, variables, expressions,* and *predefined functions.* It is the purpose of this chapter to acquaint you with these fundamental concepts.

NUMBERS

A BASIC number must be eight digits or less and may contain a decimal point and a plus or a minus sign.[1] Anything else, with the exception of E notation, is not allowed. Examples of proper and improper BASIC numbers can be seen in Table 3-1.

E NOTATION

E notation is used to represent very large or very small numbers. *To use E notation, the letter E and a positive or negative integer number not to exceed 50 is added to a BASIC number.*[2] *A decimal point in the integer number after the E is not allowed. The integer number after the E tells us how many positions or digits to move the decimal to the left, when the number is* negative, *or to the right, when the number is* positive. Table 3-2 reveals the relationship between an ordinary number and a BASIC number using E notation.

When the integer after the letter "E" is *negative,* the real number is *small* and you move the decimal to the left; when the integer is

[1] Some computer systems allow more than eight digits.

[2] For some systems the integer can be different from 50

SIC

Proper BASIC numbers	Improper BASIC numbers	Explanation
86.45	$86.45	Dollar sign is not allowed.
42000.	42,000	Comma is not allowed.
−1234567.8	−12345678.9	Too many digits—only eight are allowed not including a positive or negative sign and a decimal point.
.33333333	1/3	Slash is not allowed—this is, however, a proper *expression.*

TABLE 3-2
The use of E notation

BASIC number	*Ordinary number*	*Remark*
2.7E6	2,700,000	The decimal has been moved six places to the *right.*
2.7E-6	0.0000027	The decimal has been moved six places to the *left.*
+1.2345678E-4	0.00012345678	The decimal has been moved four places to the *left.*
−1.2345678E9	−1234567800.	The decimal has been moved nine places to the *right.*

positive, the real number is *large,* and you move the decimal to the right.

VARIABLES

A variable is symbolized by a single letter, or a single letter followed by a one-digit number (see Table 3-3).

PREDEFINED FUNCTIONS

As you will see later, BASIC provides you the flexibility of defining your own mathematical functions. Since many functions are commonly used, the functions in Table 3-4 have been predefined for your convenience.

TABLE 3-3
Examples of BASIC variables

Proper BASIC variables	*Improper BASIC variables*	*Explanation*
S	SUM	Only one letter is allowed.
T9	T10	Only a one-digit number can follow the letter.
D6	6D	The letter must be first.

TABLE 3-4 Predefined BASIC functions

*BASIC function**	*Explanation*
ABS(X)	Absolute value of X. ABS(−6) is 6.
ATN(X)	Arctangent of X in radians.†
COS(X)	Cosine of X in radians.†
EXP(X)	e^X. This is 2.718218 to the X power.
INT(X)	Integer of X. INT(8.6721) is 8.
LOG(X)	The natural logarithm of X. This logarithm uses 2.718218 as the base.
RND(X)	This generates a six-digit random number between 0 and 1. X is usually the number 1 or −1.
SIN(X)	The sine of X in radians.†
SQR(X)	The square root of X. SQR(100) is 10.
TAN(X)	The tangent of X in radians.†

*X is a number, a variable, or an expression, which will be discussed in the next section.
†For ATN(X), COS(X), SIN(X), and TAN(X), X must be in radians. A radian is 57.295 degrees. It is the angle subtended at the center of a circle by an arc along the circumference of the circle equal in length to the radius of the circle.

EXPRESSIONS

An expression is a proper combination of numbers, variables, and predefined functions. To be proper, the numbers, variables, and predefined functions must be separated by an operator. In order to be a proficient programmer, you must have:

1. The ability to recognize proper expressions.
2. The ability to evaluate expressions.
3. The ability to convert mathematical expressions to proper expressions in BASIC.

Table 3-5 lists the operators used in expressions.

In order to evaluate arithmetic expressions, you must know in what order they are performed by the computer. This hierarchy is shown in Table 3-6.

TABLE 3-5 Arithmetic operators

Operator	*Interpretation*
( )	Everything within the parentheses is evaluated before the rest of the expression takes effect on it.
** or ↑	To the power of.† 3**2 is $3^2 = 3 \times 3 = 9$. 2↑4 is $2^4 = 2 \times 2 \times 2 \times 2 = 16$.
*	Multiplication. 3*4 is $3 \times 4 = 12$.
/	Division. 3/4 = 0.75.
+ and −	Addition and subtraction.

† ↑ is not allowed on some systems.

TABLE 3-6
Hierarchy of operators

Operator	*Hierarchy*
( )	Level 1. Parentheses are always evaluated first. (3 + 2)**2 is $5^2 = 25$. Innermost parentheses are always evaluated first.
** or ↑	Level 2. Exponents are evaluated next. 3*2 ↑ 2 is 12, not 36. 2 ↑ 2 is 4; 3*4 is 12.
* and /	Level 3. Multiplication and division are next. 4 + 3*2 ↑ 2 is 16. 2 ↑ 2 is 4; 3*4 is 12; 4 + 12 is 16.
+ and –	Level 4. Addition and subtraction are done last. (4 + 2*3)*2 is 20. 2*3 is 6; 4 + 6 is 10; 10*2 is 20.

Note: When you have operators in the same level such as * and / in level 3, always evaluate from left to right. (1/2/5*16) + 0.4 is 2. 1/2 is 0.5; 0.5/5 is 0.1; 0.1*16 is 1.6; 1.6 + 0.4 is 2. 4 + 2**2**3 is 68; 2**2 is 4; 4**3 is 64; 4 + 64 is 68. Remember, addition is done last.

In evaluating arithmetic expressions, it is usually helpful to place a number corresponding to the hierarchy above each operator as seen in Table 3-7.

The final step is to learn how to convert a conventional mathematical expression into a proper expression in BASIC. This is acquired through practice. Knowledge of how to evaluate expressions is helpful in testing the expressions you have constructed. Several mathematical expressions have been converted into proper expressions in BASIC in Table 3-8.

TABLE 3-7
Evaluating arithmetic expressions (where X = 4, Y = 2, Z = 1)

Expression	*Hierarchy of operation (circled number shows order of operation)*	*Numerical value*
3 + X * Y	② ① 3 + 4 * 2	11
X + Z * Y**2	③ ② ① 4 + 1 * 2**2	8
Z/Y/X	① ② 1/2/4	0.125
(X + Y * Z) + 3 * Y	② ① ④ ③ (4 + 2 * 1) + 3 * 2	12
SQR(ABS(Z – Y * 5))	④ ③ ② ① SQR(ABS(1 – 2 * 5))	3

TABLE 3-8 Converting into arithmetic expressions in BASIC

Conventional mathematical expression	*The same expression in BASIC*
$\frac{A}{B+C}$	A/(B + C)
$\sqrt{\frac{2DC_1}{C_2}}$	SQR(2*D*C1/C2)
$(1+I)^N$	(1 + I)**N
$\frac{e^X - COS(Y+Z^2)}{SIN(X)}$	(EXP(X) – COS(Y + Z**2))/SIN(X)
$\frac{B+\sqrt{B^2-4AC}}{2A}$	(B + SQR(B**2 – 4*A*C))/(2*A)

BASIC STATEMENTS AND LINE NUMBERS

A BASIC statement has two parts, the statement number followed by a BASIC instruction. The statement number, also called a line number, must be an integer of no more than five digits, and it cannot contain plus or minus signs or decimal points.[3] Table 3-9 gives some examples.

TABLE 3-9 Statement numbers

Examples of correct statement numbers	*Typical statements*	*Examples of incorrect statement numbers*
10	10 READ X	36.7
20	20 PRINT X	+46
47	47 DATA 40	3*87
99999	99999 END	99999999

Since room should be allowed for future program modifications, you should always start with line 10 and increment each line number by 10. Thus your line numbers should be 10, 20, 30, 40, and so on. The example programs in Chapter 3 show why it is important to follow this convention. If the line numbers were 1, 2, 3, 4, and so on, *every* line would have to be rewritten for *every* modification.

REM

The REM statement permits a programmer to document a program by including *remarks.* The computer completely ignores the

[3] The number of digits may differ depending on your computer.

REM statement. After the line number and the letters REM, you insert your remark. For example:

```
10  REM R.M. STAIR 395 55 0481
20  REM THE PROGRAM NAME
```

Other REM statements should be included in your program to help other people in understanding your program. Here is an example:

```
10  REM THIS PROGRAM COMPUTES THE CIRCUMFERENCE OF A
20  REM CIRCLE WITH A DIAMETER OF 4
30  LET C=4*3.14159
40  PRINT C
50  END
```

Without REM, you may not have realized the purpose of the above program.

SUMMARY

The importance of fundamental concepts in BASIC has been stressed throughout this chapter. Every BASIC statement discussed in this book is constructed from numbers, variables, predefined functions, and expressions as Table 3-10 demonstrates.

TABLE 3-10
Examples of BASIC statements

Form	*Example*
Line # PRINT [list of expressions]	80 PRINT X,X**2†
Line # LET [Variable] = [Expression]	90 LET X = Y*SQR(Z)
Line # DATA [list of numbers]	1000 DATA 4, 5, 6
Line # GO TO line #	46 GO TO 20
Line # NEXT [variable]	100 NEXT I

†While calculations can be done using the PRINT statement, except in special circumstances, it is better to use the LET statement.

Knowledge of these fundamentals is essential. Indeed, these fundamental concepts are a prerequisite for every further chapter in this book. You may find it necessary to review this material as you progress in your studies.

Do you see how the words, PRINT, LET, DATA, GO TO, and NEXT stand out? These are *keywords;* they instruct the computer to perform a variety of tasks. The rest of this book investigates how keywords are used in constructing statements in BASIC.

QUESTIONS

3-1. Which of the following are proper numbers?

a.	47	*f.*	+87.141361
b.	.12345678	*g.*	10E1
c.	3/4	*h.*	E1
d.	−87.62	*i.*	4.6 + 8.9
e.	4,014	*j.*	−10.6E − 10

3.2. Which of the following are proper variables?

a.	X	*f.*	A
b.	X1	*g.*	4D
c.	X.2	*h.*	K9
d.	Z	*i.*	J.6
e.	SUM	*j.*	S1

3-3. Which of the following are BASIC line numbers?

a.	10	*f.*	10.5
b.	47	*g.*	17X
c.	86.1	*h.*	333
d.	3/4	*i.*	99
e.	88991	*j.*	.333

3-4. Convert the following BASIC numbers into real numbers. For example, 13E4 is 130,000.

a.	10E3	*f.*	−1E + 1
b.	3E − 3	*g.*	167486E − 6
c.	−6E − 2	*h.*	46E − 6
d.	−.02E2	*i.*	48E5
e.	.0114E3	*j.*	−4411E − 5

3-5. Evaluate the following BASIC expressions. Indicate any errors. Let A = 1, B = 3, C = 2, X = 4, Y = 5.

a.	SQR(X)	*f.*	4(B + 2*C)
b.	A + X/C	*g.*	SQR(Y + X)/3 + 4
c.	(A + X)/C	*h.*	3** INT(Y/B) + 1
d.	Y*B**C	*i.*	ABSLT(−1*Y)
e.	3X − 4Y	*j.*	(3*(1 + (4/X)*X/C)/2)

4 Writing simple programs with END, PRINT, and LET

A computer can be programmed to perform complex and sophisticated tasks in BASIC, but BASIC can be used efficiently, like a hand calculator, to make simple calculations. The approach taken in this book is to start with easier programs. First we will investigate a statement that *must* appear in every program, the END statement.

END

The END statement must be the *last* statement in every BASIC program. As seen in the example below, the END statement consists of a line number and the word END:

```
9999 END
```

The END statement performs two functions. It terminates the execution of the program, and it tells the computer system that there are no more statements in the program. Actually, an END statement by itself can be considered a BASIC program, but to get meaningful information, one more statement needs to be employed, the PRINT statement.

PRINT

The general form of the PRINT statement is:

Line # PRINT [A series of messages (enclosed in quotation marks) and/or *expressions* (each separated with a comma or a semicolon).]

Usually, the results from a PRINT statement are printed on a teletype, CRT, or similar device. Table 4-1 displays examples of proper and improper PRINT statements.

TABLE 4-1
Example PRINT statements

Proper PRINT statements	*Improper PRINT statements*	*Explanation*
10 PRINT 10	10 PRIMT 10	Misspelling.
20 PRINT Z, Y; X	20 PRINT Z: Y: X	Colons are not allowed.
30 PRINT "X IS", X	30 PRINT "X IS, X	One more quotation mark needed.
40 PRINT 3*X−Z	40 PRINT 3X−Z	Multiplication sign omitted between "3" and "X."
50 PRINT 3**2	PRINT 3**2	Missing line number.

Application 4-1

An apartment rents for $245 per month, but the current tenant will occupy the apartment for only 22 days out of 30 days of the last month before moving to a larger apartment. The following program calculates the rent for 22 days:

Program 4-1

```
10 PRINT "RENT FOR 22 DAYS IS",(22/30)*245
20 END

READY
RUNNH


RENT FOR 22 DAYS IS           179.667
```

The flowchart (Figure 4-1) for this program is also very straightforward. The computer evaluates and prints any expression, such as (22/30)*245, in addition to printing messages enclosed within quotation marks, such as "RENT FOR 22 DAYS IS".

The major two marks of punctuation in a PRINT statement are the comma (,) and the semicolon (;). As seen in the following two example programs, the comma and the semicolon determine the format of the computer output in entirely different ways.

Most computer systems use fields of 14 or 15 positions or columns per field. A comma in a PRINT statement places the next number or message to be printed in the next field. Although most computers use 15 positions, the computer that generated both example programs used 14 positions per field. Thus A is printed in column 1. Then B is printed in the next field. Since there are 14 positions per field, the next field starts in position 15. Thus B is printed in posi-

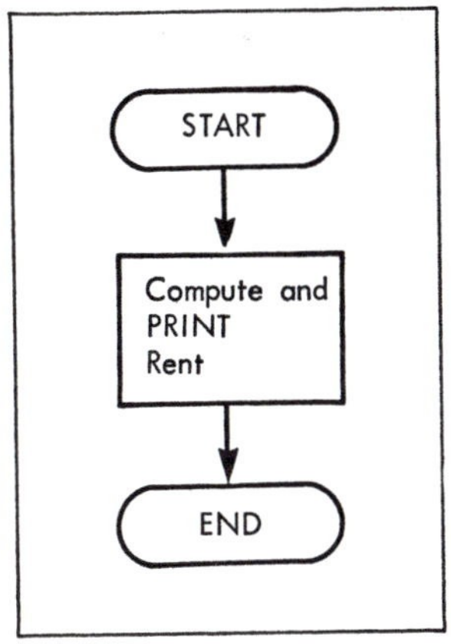

FIGURE 4-1
Flowchart for example program 4-1

tion 15. A*B is printed in the first column of the third field, which is column 29. The first two fields take 2(14) = 28 positions. When numbers are printed, one position is reserved for a minus sign.

Example program 4-1

```
10 PRINT"HERE IS WHAT A COMMA DOES IN A PRINT STATEMENT"
20 PRINT
30 PRINT"          1111111111222222222233333333334"
40 PRINT"1234567890123456789012345678901234567890"
50 PRINT
60 PRINT "A","B","A*B"
70 PRINT 3,4,3*4
80 PRINT 6,5,6*5
90 PRINT 8,-4,8*-4
100 END

READY
RUNNH


HERE IS WHAT A COMMA DOES IN A PRINT STATEMENT

          1111111111222222222233333333334
1234567890123456789012345678901234567890

A             B             A*B
 3             4             12
 6             5             30
 8            -4            -32
```

As seen in Example program 4-2, semicolons will print messages together without any spaces, and numbers will be printed with two spaces between each number. One space is reserved for a minus sign.

The use of the comma and the semicolon will be fully explored in the next two applications. Carefully study these applications.

Example program 4-2

```
10 PRINT"HERE IS WHAT A SEMICOLON DOES IN A PRINT STATEMENT"
20 PRINT
30 PRINT"MES"; "SAGE"; "S AR"; "E PRINTED TOG";"ETHER"
50 PRINT "WITHO"; "UT A"; "NY SPAC"; "ES"
60 PRINT
70 PRINT "NUMBERS ARE PRINTED WITH TWO SPACES BETWEEN THEM"
75 PRINT "ONE SPACE MAY BE USED FOR A MINUS (-) SIGN"
80 PRINT
90 PRINT 2;3;4;5;-2;-3;-4;-5
100 END

READY
RUNNH


HERE IS WHAT A SEMICOLON DOES IN A PRINT STATEMENT

MESSAGES ARE PRINTED TOGETHER
WITHOUT ANY SPACES

NUMBERS ARE PRINTED WITH TWO SPACES BETWEEN THEM
ONE SPACE MAY BE USED FOR A MINUS (-) SIGN

 2  3  4  5 -2 -3 -4 -5
```

Application 4-2

Leslie Moore has been asked to write a program to generate a table of numbers, their squares, and their square roots. The numbers are 1, 2, 3, 4, and 5.

Program 4-2

```
1 REM LESLIE MOORE
5  REM SQUARE ROOT TABLE
10 PRINT "SQUARE ROOT TABLE"
20 PRINT
25 PRINT "---------------------------------------"
30 PRINT "X","SQUARE ROOT","X SQUARED"
40 PRINT "---------------------------------------"
50 PRINT 1, SQR (1), 1**2
60 PRINT 2, SQR (2), 2**2
70 PRINT 3, SQR (3), 3**2
80 PRINT 4, SQR (4), 4**2
90 PRINT 5,  "   " , 5**2
100 PRINT "---------------------------------------"
110 END

READY
RUNNH


SQUARE ROOT TABLE

---------------------------------------
X            SQUARE ROOT   X SQUARED
---------------------------------------
1            1             1
2            1.41421       4
3            1.73205       9
4            2             16
5                          25
---------------------------------------
```

Several very important concepts are shown in the above program; they should be carefully studied.

1. *A PRINT statement will print any message in quotation marks and any number, variable, or expression.* See lines 10, 30, 40, 50, 60, 70, 80, 90, and 100.
2. As seen in line 20, *a PRINT statement with nothing after it will cause the computer to skip to the beginning of the next line* to create spacing for clarity and attractiveness. In a sense, it is printing a line of *nothing.*
3. A comma will give you normal spacing. In fact, *the comma will put one message or expression in one field of 14 or 15 spaces.* It is almost like a tab on a typewriter set at 0, 15, 30, 45, and so on.
4. " " in a PRINT statement will cause the computer to skip to the next field in the line as seen in line 90 and in the next-to-the-last output line. In a sense, " " in a PRINT statement tells the computer system to print a *blank* message. It is like hitting the tab key on a typewriter to skip over a field. Two commas together (,,) will also skip over a field for some computers.

The PRINT statement has some other features that will be especially useful in later chapters. These features are introduced to you in the following application.

Application 4-3

The following program is presented to show you some of the special format options of the PRINT statement.

Program 4-3

```
10 PRINT "APP";
20 PRINT "ENDIX I"
30 PRINT
40 PRINT "INT"; "EREST",
50 PRINT "CAL"; "CULATION"
60 PRINT
70 PRINT .07; 2; (1+.07)**2,
80 PRINT "ARE I, N, AND (1+I";
90 PRINT ")**N"
100 END

READY
RUNNH


APPENDIX I

INTEREST      CALCULATION

 0.07  2  1.1449             ARE I, N, AND (1+I)**N
```

Although this program would never be written in practice, it is given here to show you how commas and semicolons may be used. These two marks of punctuation have a special meaning in a PRINT statement as outlined below:

1. As seen at the end of line 40 and line 70, *a comma at the end of a PRINT statement causes whatever is printed in the next PRINT statement to be printed on the* same *line.* See the last two lines of output. This is useful when there is not enough room in one print statement.
2. The semicolon gives compact spacing. Line 40 again reveals that *two messages separated with a semicolon are printed together,* and line 70 shows that *expressions separated by a semicolon are printed with only two spaces between them* (one of the two spaces is sometimes used for a minus sign). As seen in line 80 and in the last output line, a semicolon at the *end* of a PRINT statement causes the next message or expression in the next PRINT statement to be printed on the *same* line.

When many calculations are to be performed, the PRINT statement can be awkward. The PRINT statement is most cumbersome when the results of one calculation are used in another calculation. Computations from a PRINT statement are *not* stored in the computer's memory. The solution to this problem is to place some of the intermediate or more complex computations in a separate statement, the LET statement. Computations made in a LET statement *are* stored in the computer's memory.

LET

The LET statement is the workhorse of BASIC; its main purpose is to simplify complex or interrelated calculations. Although calculations can be performed in other BASIC statements, such as the PRINT statement, most processing is done using the LET statement. The LET statement, which has an appearance similar to that of an algebraic equation, is used to *assign* or *define* a variable to be equal in value to an expression. The LET statement is *not* an equation that we attempt to solve for some unknown quantity. *The LET statement is a definition that assigns a value or a number to a variable.*

```
40 LET X = 4*10 - 1
50 LET X = X + 10
```

In line 40, X is assigned a value of 39, and in line 50, X is reassigned a value of 49(39 + 10). Remember, you are *not* solving for anything in a LET statement. The LET statement is a definition.

LET statements have the following form:

line # LET [variable] = [expression]

As can be seen in Figure 4-2, LET statements are executed sequentially and the value of several variables can be used in assigning new variables. It should be pointed out that all BASIC statements will be executed sequentially according to the numerical order of the statement numbers. Some computer systems allow the word "LET" to be omitted. When complex calculations are to be made, the LET statement can be used to break down a complex expression into several smaller and easier-to-understand expressions.

FIGURE 4-2

a. 40 LET X = 1↑2↑3
b. 50 LET Y = 2*X
c. 60 LET Z = Y + X
d. 70 LET X = Z – Y + 4

The following assignments are made.

a. X is assigned a value of 1 in line 40.
b. Y is assigned a value of 2 (because 2*1 = 2) in line 50.
c. Z is assigned a value of 3 (because 2 + 1 = 3) in line 60.
d. X is assigned a value of 5 (because 3 – 2 + 4 = 5) in line 70. The value of 1, assigned to X in line 40, is replaced with the number 5.

Application 4-4

B. Larsen, for a class assignment, must prepare a flowchart and write a program to solve quadratic equations of the following form:

$$AX^2 + BX + C = 0.$$

To solve for the values of X (the roots of the equation), the equation below can be used:

$$X = \frac{-B \pm \sqrt{B^2 - 4AC}}{2A}$$

where

$$B^2 - 4AC > 0.$$

For example, here is how a quadratic equation can be solved:

$$X^2 + 3X + 2 = 0.$$

In this case, A = 1, B = 3, and C = 2. A is the coefficient of X^2; B is the coefficient of X, and C is the constant. Now we can solve for X:

$$X = \frac{-B \pm \sqrt{B^2 - 4AC}}{2A} = \frac{-3 \pm \sqrt{3^2 - (4)(1)(2)}}{(2)(1)}$$

$$= \frac{-3 \pm \sqrt{9-8}}{2} = \frac{-3+1}{2} \quad \text{or} \quad \frac{-3-1}{2};$$

$$X = -1 \quad \text{or} \quad -2.$$

If you wish, you can plug these numbers into the quadratic equation as a check.

The program should adhere to the following requirements:

1. Desired output.
   The two values for X should be the output for this program. The output should appear as follows:

   THE VALUES OF X ARE XXX AND XXX

   where XXX is the appropriate number.
2. Input data required.
   The data will be supplied through LET statements.

   2 should be assigned to A
   4 should be assigned to B
   1 should be assigned to C

The flowchart for this program appears on page 37.

Program 4-4 was developed from this flowchart. This program is one of many programs that will generate the desired output. Note that line 60 is an intermediate step that simplifies the computations in lines 70 and 80.

In larger programs, it can be very difficult to keep track of what is happening in all the LET statements. You can imagine how difficult it is to remember all of the values assigned to the variables if we have more than a few statements. Very few students, for example, could remember all of the values contained in 50 LET statements. The

Program 4-4

```
10 REM B. LARSEN
20 REM QUADRATIC EQUATION
30 LET A = 2
40 LET B = 4
50 LET C = 1
60 LET S = SQR(B ↑ 2 - 4 * A * C)
70 LET X1 = (-B + S) / (2 * A)
80 LET X2 = (-B - S) / (2 * A)
90 PRINT "THE VALUES OF X ARE", X1, "AND", X2
100 END

READY
RUNNH


THE VALUES OF X ARE         -0.292893     AND          -1.70711
```

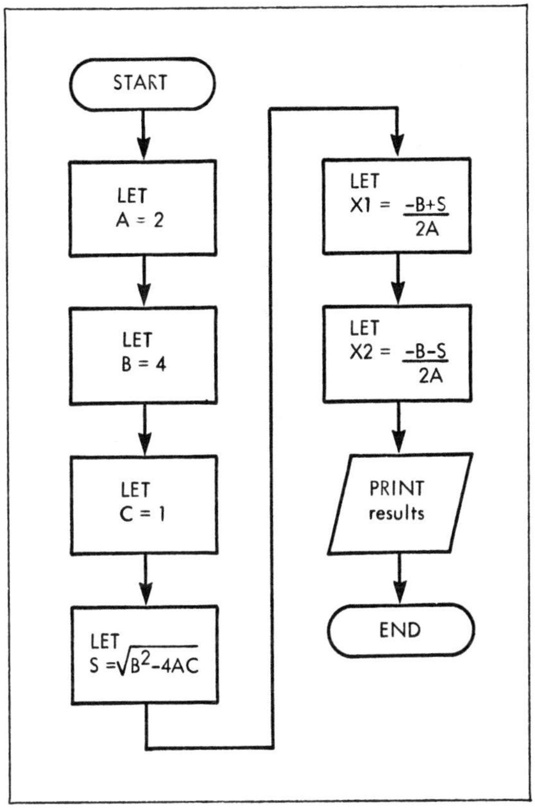

computer, of course, stores all the values assigned to variables automatically.

In writing, testing, and debugging computer programs, it is very helpful if the programmer has a way of systematically recording values assigned to variables. This can be accomplished by setting aside a storage area similar in structure and operation to a storage area in a computer system. The following two examples will reveal this process.

```
40 LET X = 1↑2↑3
50 LET Y = 2*X
60 LET Z = Y+X
70 LET X = Z-Y+4
80 LET A = X+Y+Z
```

The *storage area* on page 38 graphically follows the execution of the above statements. In line 40, 1 is assigned to X; in line 50, 2 is assigned to Y; and in line 60, 3 is assigned to Z. In line 70, 5 is

Storage area (memory)

X	
Line no.	*Value*
40 70	~~1~~ 5

Y	
Line no.	*Value*
50	2

Z	
Line no.	*Value*
60	3

A	
Line no.	*Value*
80	10

assigned to X. The previous assignment for X, which was 1, is eliminated; thus it has been crossed out in the storage area. In line 80, A is assigned a value of 10.

```
 10 LET X7 = 4 – 2
 20 LET A = X7↑2
 30 LET Z = A – 13
 40 LET X7 = ABS(Z)
 50 LET X7 = SQR(X7)
 60 LET A = –A
 70 LET Z = 2↑(7 + A)
 80 LET X = X7 + A + Z
 90 LET A = A**2
100 LET X = X7 + A + Z
```

The values shown on the next page were obtained by sequentially analyzing or executing each statement in a fashion similar to what we would expect the computer to do. The results can be summarized in the following table (these results are here to help us analyze what the computer is doing).

Normally the above calculations can be made mentally. Then the appropriate assignments are placed in the storage area. We usually do not need to construct the table unless the statements are complex and numerous. If you are wondering what happened to the other values for X7, A, Z, and X, they were all subsequently replaced and lost forever. A variable can only be assigned *one* value at any one time.

Storage area (memory)

X7	
Line no.	*Value*
10	~~2~~
40	~~9~~
50	3

A	
Line no.	*Value*
20	~~4~~
60	~~−4~~
90	16

Z	
Line no.	*Value*
30	~~−9~~
70	8

X	
Line no.	*Value*
80	~~7~~
100	27

Sequential execution of statements

Line no.	*Action*
10	4 − 2 = 2; 2 assigned to X7
20	2↑2 = 4; 4 assigned to A
30	4 − 13 = −9; −9 assigned to Z
40	ABS(−9) = 9; 9 assigned to X7
50	SQR(9) = 3; 3 assigned to X7
60	−A = −4; −4 assigned to A
70	2↑(7 − 4) = 8; 8 assigned to Z
80	3 − 4 + 8 = 7; 7 assigned to X
90	−4↑2 = 16; 16 assigned to A
100	3 + 16 + 8 = 27; 27 assigned to X

A POSSIBLE ERROR: UNDEFINED VARIABLES

Consider the following computer program:

```
10 LET X = 10
20 LET T = T + X
30 PRINT T
40 END
```

In line 20, the variable T in the expression is *undefined* because a value has not been assigned to it. In some computer systems, undefined variables are assigned a value of 0; thus the output of the program would be the number 10. Other computer systems do not allow undefined variables; thus an error message would result. In this book, we will avoid this problem by setting all possible undefined variables equal to 0 in LET statements at the beginning of the program like "5 LET T = 0." This type of statement can be eliminated if your computer system allows undefined variables.

A pattern, or a series of statements repeated several times, is very common in programming. Following is another example of a program that has a pattern.

Application 4-5

A very popular way of depreciating an asset, such as a building, is double declining balance. The depreciation in any year is calculated as follows:

$$\text{Depreciation this year} = \frac{2}{\text{Useful life in years}} \times \text{Value of asset this year}$$

where

$$\text{Value of asset this year} = \text{Value of asset last year} - \text{Depreciation last year}$$

For example, a building with a value of \$100,000 and a useful life of 20 years can be depreciated using double declining balance, giving the following results for the first three years:

$$\text{D} = \text{Depreciation in any year;}$$
$$\text{V} = \text{Value in any year.}$$

$$D_{\text{1st year}} = \frac{2}{20}(100{,}000) = \underline{\$10{,}000};$$

$$V_{\text{2d year}} = \$100{,}000 - \$10{,}000 = \$90{,}000;$$

$$D_{\text{2d year}} = \frac{2}{20}(90{,}000) = \underline{\$9{,}000};$$

$$V_{\text{3d year}} = \$90{,}000 - \$9{,}000 = \$81{,}000;$$

$$D_{\text{3d year}} = \frac{2}{20}(81{,}000) = \underline{\$8{,}100}$$

Write a program to calculate depreciation using double declining balance over four years.

A. Desired output

The output should be as follows:

```
DOUBLE DECLINING BALANCE

YEAR          DEPRECIATION
1ST               XXXX
2ND               XXXX
3RD               XXXX
4TH               XXXX
```

where XXXX is the appropriate number.

B. Required data

The asset, a building, has an initial value of $187,000 and a useful life of 22 years.

C. Program

Program 4-5 is one that will give the desired output.

To understand the operation of the above program, study the execution of each statement.

Although there are many ways of writing the above program using a combination of LET and PRINT statements, there are more effi-

Program 4-5

```
10 REM W. LANGE
20 REM DOUBLE DECLINING BALANCE
30 PRINT "DOUBLE DECLINING BALANCE"
40 PRINT
50 PRINT "YEAR", "AMOUNT"
55 REM 1ST YEAR DEPRECIATION
60 LET V = 187000
70 LET D = (2/22)*V
80 PRINT "1ST", D
85 REM 2ND YEAR DEPRECIATION
90 LET V = V - D
100 LET D = (2/22)*V
110 PRINT "2ND", D
115 REM 3RD YEAR DEPRECIATION
120 LET V = V - D
130 LET D = (2/22)*V
140 PRINT "3RD", D
145 REM 4TH YEAR DEPRECIATION
150 LET V = V - D
160 LET D = (2/22)*V
170 PRINT "4TH", D
180 END

READY
RUNNH


DOUBLE DECLINING BALANCE

YEAR           AMOUNT
1ST             17000
2ND             15454.5
3RD             14049.6
4TH             12772.4
```

cient ways of doing the same thing by reading in the data and using a loop in the program. This will be fully discussed in the next two chapters.

Sequential execution of statements

Line no.	*Action*
10	Print programmer name
20	Print program name
30	Print a heading
40	Skip a line
50	Print a heading
55	(Remark)
60	Define initial value of asset: $187,000
70	Calculate 1st year depreciation
80	Print 1st year depreciation
85	(Remark)
90	Calculate value of asset (for 2d year
100	Calculate depreciation for 2d year
110	Print 2d year depreciation
115	(Remark)
120	Calculate value of asset for 3d year
130	Calculate depreciation for 3d year
140	Print 3d year depreciation
145	(Remark)
150	Calculate value of asset for 4th year
160	Calculate depreciation for 4th year
170	Print 4th year depreciation
180	Terminate program

SUMMARY

In this chapter we have investigated the proper form and the appropriate use of the END, PRINT, and LET statements. As seen in the chapter, programs can be written using only LET statements, PRINT statements, and the END statement. Although complicated programs can be written using these statements, these programs would most likely be very inefficient, long, and cumbersome. In future chapters, easier and more efficient ways of writing programs discussed in this chapter will be revealed. In addition, we will learn how to instruct the computer system to perform literally thousands of calculations in programs that may contain less than a dozen statements.

QUESTIONS

4-1. What is the purpose of the END statement?

4-2. Which of the following PRINT statements contain one or more grammatical errors? Correct these errors. There is more than one way.

a. 10 PRINT X
b. 46 PRINT 46
c. 40 "PRINT Z"
d. 15 PRINT 3X
e. 20 PRINT "ANSWER"
f. PRINT "X IS", X
g. 60 PRINT 3*H
h. 100 PRINT 4 + 6 =
i. 90 PRINT SQR(A – 4*B)
j. 30 PRINT 1,421.20

4-3. Which of the following LET statements have one or more grammatical errors? Correct these errors. There may be many ways.

a. 10 LET Z = 4
b. 20 LET X = SUM
c. 40 LET T = T – 1
d. 50 LET X + 4 = 6
e. 60 LET 7 = X + 2
f. 30 LET K = 1, J = 17
g. 40 LET Z = Z – Z
h. 50 LET K EQUAL 17 – 1
i. 60 LET B = <14*H
j. 70 LET L = L

4-4. What is stored in memory or main storage as a result of the following statements?

a.
```
10 LET X = 17
20 LET Y = (X - 9)/3
```

b.
```
10 LET B = 4*2 - 3
20 LET C = B - 1
30 LET D = SQR(B**2 - C**2)
```

c.
```
10 LET K = 6
20 LET T = 0
30 LET L = INT(K/5)
40 LET L = L + 1
50 LET T = T + L
70 LET K = K + T + L
```

4-5. Write a number to print your name, student number, and course number.

4-6. Write a program to find the area of a circle. The radius is four inches. The formula is: Area = (3.14159)(square of radius).

Writing realistic and useful programs with READ, INPUT, GO TO, IF, and ON–GO TO

5

How inconvenient it would be to change a bunch of LET statements each time you wanted to run a program with different data. You would have to rummage through larger programs to locate all the LET statements that needed to be changed, and then you would have to be very careful to make just the right changes to insert the new values and get rid of the old values. With only the END statement and a few PRINT statements remaining unchanged, it could be easier to rewrite the entire program each time new data is used. A simple solution to this problem would be to keep all the data in one part of the program and then to read in values to be processed when they are needed.

READ AND DATA STATEMENTS

Seldom are programs written to be run just once. *READ and DATA statements are used when a program is to be run more than once. The values are placed in DATA statements and assigned to variables in READ statements during the execution of the program. READ and DATA statements have the following form:*

line # READ [a list of variables]
line # DATA [a list of numbers][1]

Application 5-1

The United States is one of the few countries not using the metric system, but conversion to metric seems inevitable. Program 5-1 converts feet to meters and centimeters.

[1] This form will be modified in a later chapter.

Program 5-1

```
10 REM L LOPEZ
20 REM FROM FEET(F) TO METERS(M) AND CENTIMETERS(C)
30 READ F
40 LET C = F*30.48
50 LET M = F*.3048
60 PRINT "FEET","CENTIMETERS","METERS"
70 PRINT F,C,M
100 DATA 7
9999 END

READY
RUNNH


FEET           CENTIMETERS   METERS
 7              213.36         2.1336
```

The flowchart appears in Figure 5-1.

Program 5-1 converts seven feet to centimeters and meters. Any time you want to run the program using something other than seven feet, only the number in the DATA statement needs to be changed.

When you are reading several variables, care should be taken to ensure that the number of variables assigned in one or more READ statements is equal to the number of numbers or constants in one or more DATA statements. A surplus of numbers is ignored by the computer, but insufficient data results in an "out-of-data" error message,

FIGURE 5-1

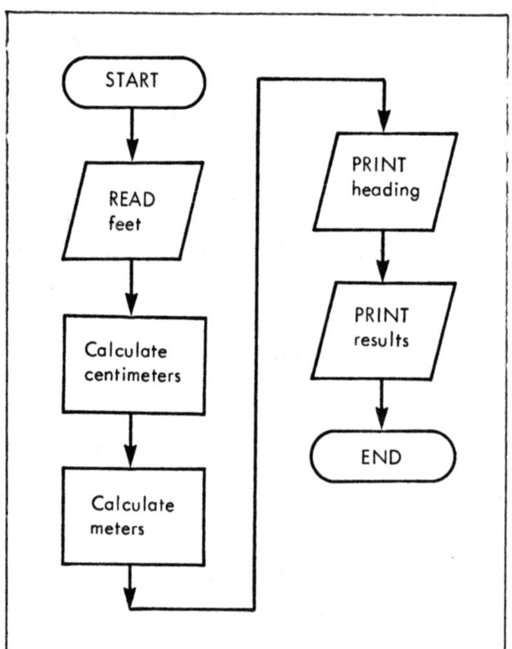

and the computer immediately stops execution. During program execution, the first variable in the first READ statement is assigned to the first number in the first DATA statement, the second variable to the second number, and so forth.

All variables in READ statements and all numbers in DATA statements are separated by commas. Although DATA statements can be placed anywhere in the program, they are customarily placed near the end.

It should be emphasized that the numbers placed in one or more DATA statements must be in the order corresponding to the order of variables supplied by READ statements. The number of DATA statements used, however, is not of importance. In most computer systems, all of the numbers in DATA statements are taken in order and placed in the computer's memory in one large data block before the program is executed. During program execution, variables in READ statements will be set equal to the numbers previously stored in the data block in the computer's memory. For example, if you wanted to store the numbers 6, 23, 45, and –9 in the computer's memory, any one of the following sets of DATA statements would work. See Table 5-1.

It is easy to use a BASIC program written by someone else if you know BASIC and if the program employs READ and DATA statements. You change a few DATA statements and RUN the program. Someone not knowing BASIC can learn to do this, but there is an easier way of inputting a limited amount of data without ever changing the program.

INPUT

The INPUT statement accepts data directly from the terminal during program execution. DATA statements are not needed. When the computer encounters an INPUT statement, it prints a question mark and waits for you to type in the data. How convenient!

TABLE 5-1 Examples of DATA statements

Statement	*Block of data in computer's memory*
100 DATA 6, 23, 45, –9	6, 23, 45, –9
100 DATA 6, 23 110 DATA 45, –9	6, 23, 45, –9
100 DATA 6 110 DATA 23 120 DATA 45, –9	6, 23, 45, –9

Application 5-2

With the ever increasing price of gasoline, Eric Lange would like to write a program (to be used by people not familiar with any computer programming language) that calculates miles per gallon and cost per mile. The data is 318 miles, 18.7 gallons, and $1.50/gallon. See Program 5-2.

Program 5-2

```
10 REM E. LANGE
20 REM MILES/GAL AND COST/MILE
30 PRINT "THIS PROGRAM COMPUTES MILES/GAL AND COST/MILE"
40 PRINT "PLEASE ENTER TOTAL MILES, TOTAL GALLONS AND COST/GALLON";
50 INPUT M,G,C
60 PRINT
70 PRINT "MILES/GAL = ",M/G
80 PRINT "COST/MILE = ",G*C/M
90 END

READY
RUNNH


THIS PROGRAM COMPUTES MILES/GAL AND COST/MILE
PLEASE ENTER TOTAL MILES, TOTAL GALLONS AND COST/GALLON ?318,18.7,1.50

MILES/GAL =     17.0053
COST/MILE =     8.82075E-2
```

The INPUT statement in line 50 takes the place of a READ and DATA statement. Of course, it is helpful to have line 40. Indeed, it is always wise to have an explantory PRINT statement preceding an INPUT statement, otherwise the computer would print only a question mark and then wait for a response. An inexperienced computer user, seeing the lonely question mark, would probably mutter, "This dumb machine is more confused than I am." You may note the semicolon at the end of line 40. As you would expect, this causes the question mark to be printed on the same line with the message.

INPUT statements are easy to use, interactive, and conversational. You don't have to change any part of the program to use new data. With all these advantages, why would you ever use READ and DATA statements? Consider a larger program with several input statements containing over 50 variables. One mistake in entering the data usually provokes muffled profanity from the user because most programs do not provide a means for correcting data input mistakes, and the program must be run again with care to ensure that *all* data is entered correctly. With READ and DATA statements, a mistake can be corrected by changing one line in the program. Thus, when a large amount of data is used in a program, READ and DATA statements may be more efficient than, and preferable to, INPUT statements.

Now, suppose you wanted to run several sets of data through the same program at one time. If READ and DATA statements are employed, you run the program for each new set of data. With 100 data sets, for example, you would change the DATA statement, type RUN, and hit the carriage return key 100 times. Typing the word RUN 100 times in itself would be boring. It is also unnecessary when a GO TO statement is employed.

GO TO

The GO TO statement is powerful. With it, you can branch to any part of the program during execution—even to the beginning of the program to process another set of data. Here is the form of the GO TO statement:

line #1 GO TO line #2

(Line #1 is the number of the GO TO statement, and line #2 is the number of the statement next executed as the result of the GO TO statement.)

Application 5-3

Certain items will be sold at a 20 percent discount during the annual sale. The following program prints the item number, retail price, amount of discount, and the discount price for each item.

Program 5-3

```
10 REM R. STUART
20 REM PRICE DISCOUNT
30 REM I=ITEM NO,P=PRICE,D=DISCOUNT,S=DISCOUNT PRICE
40 PRINT "ITEM NO","PRICE","DISCOUNT","DISCOUNT PRICE"
50 READ I,P
60 LET D = P*.2
70 LET S = P - D
80 PRINT I,P,D,S
90 GO TO 50
100 REM EACH LINE OF DATA CONTAINS I AND P FOR AN ITEM
110 DATA 100,59.95
120 DATA 101,9.75
130 DATA 106,25
140 DATA 120,109.9
150 DATA 104,36.25
9999 END

READY
RUNNH
```

```
ITEM NO        PRICE          DISCOUNT       DISCOUNT PRICE
 100            59.95          11.99          47.96
 101            9.75           1.95           7.8
 106            25             5              20
 120            109.9          21.98          87.92
 104            36.25          7.25           29

? OUT OF DATA IN LINE 50
```

The flowchart displayed in Figure 5-2 reveals the power of the GO TO statement. Notice the line that starts before the END statement and goes to the READ statement. This is a *loop.* It is created by the GO TO statement.

The GO TO statement in line 90 creates a loop that reads data in line 50, makes the appropriate calculations in lines 60 and 70, and prints the results in line 80. If data for 1,000 items were included in DATA statements, this program would loop 1,000 times—reading, calculating, and printing the results. This program will continue until there is no more data, and then an "out-of-data" error message will be printed. At this stage, don't worry about this error message because all of the results will be printed before it is printed.

FIGURE 5-2

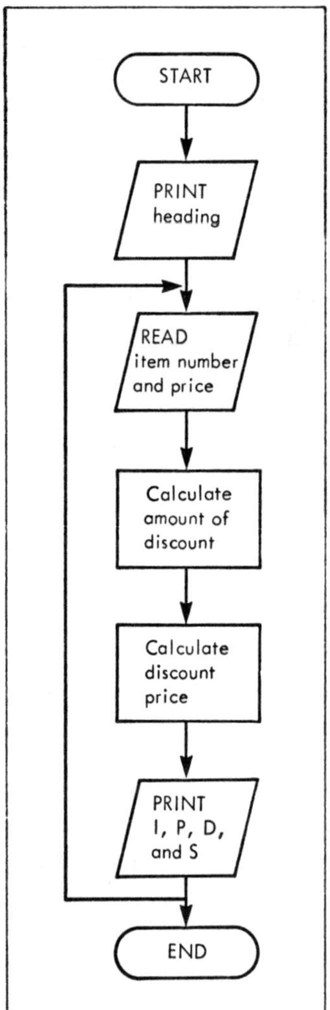

Study the above program; it has an often used structure. Observe line 40; it prints a heading under which all the results appear. Notice that this statement precedes the loop. Try to see the similarity in structure between the above program and the next program.

Application 5-4

R. Barry would like to write a program to calculate and print running totals and averages for daily sales in thousands of dollars.

Again, the instructions that are to be executed once are placed before or after the loop. In this program, the heading in line 30 and the LET statements in line 50 and 60 appear before the loop. The loop includes the statements in line 70 through line 120.

Perhaps you are having difficulty understanding how this program works. If so, you may wish to study what is happening in the computer's memory. If you understand how this program works, you might want to skip over Table 5-2 and explanation.

Carefully analyze the structure of line 80 and line 90. Line 80 counts from 0 to 7, and line 90 accumulates the values of X. N and T could be replaced in all the appropriate lines by any other variables, and the program would still work.

The loop created in Application 5-4 reads data and calculates and prints the average and total for every number. If you want the aver-

Program 5-4

```
10 REM R. BARRY
20 REM TOTALS AND AVERAGES
30 PRINT "DATA","NUMBER","TOTAL","AVERAGE"
40 REM X=DATA,N=NUMBER,T=TOTAL,A=AVERAGE
50 LET N = 0
60 LET T = 0
70 READ X
80 LET N = N + 1
90 LET T = T + X
100 LET A = T / N
110 PRINT X,N,T,A
120 GO TO 70
130 DATA 6,10,8,6
140 DATA 5,15,10.64
9999 END

READY
RUNNH

DATA          NUMBER        TOTAL         AVERAGE
 6             1             6             6
 10            2             16            8
 8             3             24            8
 6             4             30            7.5
 5             5             35            7
 15            6             50            8.33333
 10.64         7             60.64         8.66286

? OUT OF DATA IN LINE 70
```

age and total for all the numbers and nothing else, then you don't want all of those intermediate averages and totals that the above program prints. Only the last total and average should be printed. Unfortunately, with what has been presented so far, a convenient way does not exist. Ideally line 110, which prints the results, should be placed outside and below the loop. IF the last data value is encountered, *then* the computer should leave the loop and print the total and average for all of the numbers once.

IF

Like the GO TO statement, the IF statement is powerful. *The IF statement will cause the computer to branch to another line number only if certain relationships are true; otherwise, the computer ignores the statement and proceeds to the next statement in the program.*

Before we discuss any applications, you should learn how to construct proper IF statements. Most computers allow two general forms that do the same thing. They are given on the next page.

TABLE 5-2

Storage area (memory)

X		
Line no.	*Value*	*Printed?*
70	6	1st loop
70	10	2d loop
70	8	3d loop
70	6	4th loop
70	5	5th loop
70	15	6th loop
70	10.64	7th loop
70	out-of-data	

N		
Line no.	*Value*	*Printed?*
50	0	no
80	1	1st loop
80	2	2d loop
80	3	3d loop
80	4	4th loop
80	5	5th loop
80	6	6th loop
80	7	7th loop

T		
Line no.	*Value*	*Printed?*
60	0	no
90	6	1st loop
90	16	2d loop
90	24	3d loop
90	30	4th loop
90	35	5th loop
90	50	6th loop
90	60.64	7th loop

A		
Line no.	*Value*	*Printed?*
100	6	1st loop
100	8	2d loop
100	8	3d loop
100	7.5	4th loop
100	7	5th loop
100	8.33333	6th loop
100	8.662856	7th loop

line #1 IF [Expression] [Relationship] [Expression] GO TO line #2
line #1 IF [Expression] [Relationship] [Expression] THEN line #2

Expressions and how they are constructed have been discussed, but what is a *relationship* in BASIC? Table 5-3 answers this question.

If the relationship is true the computer goes to the appropriate line number, but if the relationship does not hold, then the computer proceeds to the next line number.

Be very careful to write IF statements as indicated above. Deviations from the above general form will usually result in an error message. For example the relationship "<=" is correct, but most computers will not permit the reverse, "=<".

Here is an application that uses the IF statement.

TABLE 5-3
Relationships used in IF statements

Meaning	*Symbol*	*Example*
Less than	<	10 IF X<7 THEN 65
Greater than	>	40 IF X−4>Z*2 THEN 70
Equal to	=	35 IF Z=17 GO TO 20
Less than or equal to	<=	60 IF A<=B**2 THEN 40
Greater than or equal to	>=	45 IF SQR(X)>=D GO TO 21
Not equal to	<>	70 IF 3<>Z GO TO 10

Application 5-5

An employee is paid twice the normal rate for all hours worked over 40 hours for any given week. Program 5-5 calculates gross pay including overtime.

After the computer reads the data, the computer determines in line 40 if the total hours worked are less than or equal to 40. If so, the computer goes to line 70 to compute gross pay by multiplying hours worked times the pay rate. If the hours worked exceed 40, the computer drops down to line 45, where the number of overtime hours is computed. Gross pay is set equal to 40 times the pay rate plus the number of overtime hours multiplied by twice the normal pay rate. Make a special note of the GO TO statement in line 60. What would happen if line 60 were omitted from the program? The employer would like line 60 to be left out, but the employees would be outraged. Omitting line 60 would cause the computer to recalculate gross pay, G, in line 70, and nobody would be paid double time for working more than 40 hours.

Program 5-5

```
10 REM ED BUFFINGTON
20 REM GROSS PAY
25 PRINT "EMPLOYEE NO.","HOURS","PAY RATE","GROSS PAY"
30 READ N,H,R
40 IF H <= 40 THEN 70
44 REM H1 IS NUMBER OF HOURS OVER 40
45 LET H1 = H - 40
50 LET G = 40 * R + H1 * R * 2
60 GO TO 80
70 LET G = H * R
80 PRINT N,H,R,G
85 GO TO 30
90  REM NO., HOURS AND RATE OF EACH WORKER
100 DATA 100,40,5.5
110 DATA 101,40,5
120 DATA 102,35,5
130 DATA 103,45,5
140 DATA 104,100,5.5
150 DATA 105,31,5.5
9999 END

READY
RUNNH


EMPLOYEE NO.  HOURS         PAY RATE      GROSS PAY
 100           40            5.5           220
 101           40            5             200
 102           35            5             175
 103           45            5             250
 104           100           5.5           880
 105           31            5.5           170.5

? OUT OF DATA IN LINE 30
```

We have just explored several ways an IF statement can be used. But the IF statement has a far more important function when the output of the program is used for decision making. The IF statement is a powerful tool in decision making when used in the context of management by exception. This concept focuses on those situations that are out of the ordinary or *exceptional.* These circumstances usually require immediate and corrective action on the part of the decision maker. The supply of a miracle drug in a hospital is too low. A bank loan is four months overdue. An employee is taking advantage of a company by reporting too much overtime. If a computer system is used, the necessary programs should be written to alert decision makers to potential or existing problems. Reports from a computer that contain information revealing situations that are out of the ordinary or exceptional are called "exception reports."

ON–GO TO

The IF statement causes the computer to follow one of two possible branches. *The ON–GO TO statement allows many branches or alternative paths.* Although several IF statements could be combined to produce the same results, the ON–GO TO statement is more efficient. ON–GO TO statements have the following form:

line # ON [EXPRESSION] GO TO 1st line #, 2d line #, etc.

When the computer encounters this statement, it takes the integer of the expression first; for example, 1.78 becomes 1. Then if this value is 1, the computer goes to the first line number; if it is 2, the computer goes to the second line number, and so forth. If there are not enough line numbers after GO TO, the computer goes to the next line.

There are many applications of the ON–GO TO statement. Here is one that is being used by an increasing number of schools.

Application 5-6

In addition to complex business applications and sophisticated scientific applications, the computer has been used as an instruc-

Program 5-6

```
10 PRINT "WHAT IS THE VALUE OF (1 + 2**3)/1 + 1"
15 PRINT
20 PRINT " "," 1)  28  "
30 PRINT " "," 2)  10  "
40 PRINT " "," 3)  4.5 "
50 PRINT " "," 4)  14  "
60 PRINT " "," 5)  NONE OF THE ABOVE  "
70 INPUT X
80 ON X,GO TO 100,130,160,190,220
90 PRINT "ENTER 1, 2, 3, 4, OR 5"
100 PRINT "NO. EXPONENTS, SUCH AS 2**3";
110 PRINT " ARE DONE FIRST. TRY AGAIN"
120 GO TO 70
130 PRINT "YES. 2**3 = 8; (1+8) = (9)"
140 PRINT "(9)/1 = 9; 9+1 = 10."
150 GO TO 240
160 PRINT "NO, DIVISION IS DONE BEFORE"
170 PRINT "ADDITION. TRY AGAIN"
180 GO TO 70
190 PRINT "NO, YOU HAVE MADE SEVERAL ";
200 PRINT "MISTAKES. TRY AGAIN."
210 GO TO 70
220 PRINT "NO. TRY AGAIN"
230 GO TO 70
240 END

READY
RUNNH


WHAT IS THE VALUE OF (1 + 2**3)/1 + 1

              1)  28
              2)  10
              3)  4.5
              4)  14
              5)  NONE OF THE ABOVE
 ?5
NO. TRY AGAIN
 ?1
NO. EXPONENTS, SUCH AS 2**3 ARE DONE FIRST. TRY AGAIN
 ?2
YES. 2**3 = 8; (1+8) = (9)
(9)/1 = 9; 9+1 = 10.
```

tional aid for students of all ages. This type of activity is called *Computer Aided Instruction* (CAI).

Assume that the computer has instructed a student, using PRINT statements, how to evaluate a BASIC expression. Program 5-6 tests the student on these concepts.

In most CAI programs, there are many questions like the one in Program 5-6. Usually these questions follow instructional material contained in PRINT statements. These programs can be extremely flexible. If one or more questions are answered incorrectly, then the computer can print more instructional material followed by more questions. This approach to instruction has been used in almost every field of study.

SUMMARY

When a computer program is to be run several times using different data, this data should be entered into the computer using READ and DATA or INPUT statements. The GO TO statement can be used to create loops or to branch to another part of the program. Although the above statements are essential, the IF statement is one of the most versatile and powerful statements in BASIC. Loops, branching, and exception reports are just a few uses of the IF statement.

At the beginning of this book, it was mentioned that it is easier to *learn* the rules of BASIC than *how* to use the rules to write good BASIC programs. Indeed it is easier to learn how each chess piece moves than it is to become a grand master. Before you proceed to the next chapter, you may wish to review how the statements in this chapter were used to construct computer programs.

QUESTIONS

5-1. Write a program to *read* three numbers and print the average. Use 37.62, 86.4618, and –42.31 for your data.

5-2. Write a program to *input* three numbers and print the average. Use the data given in 5-1 above.

5-3. Professor G. White has given three tests, and would like to talk to all students whose grade average is below 65. Write a program to generate a list of these students and their averages given the following data:

Student	*Test 1*	*Test 2*	*Test 3*
1	66	42	86
2	47	81	86
3	60	80	84
4	86	50	55
5	76	85	86
6	41	60	82
7	90	80	65
8	67	59	76
9	72	68	51
10	80	71	52

5-4. Holding Right, Inc., a small publisher, offers the following royalties to authors:

Royalties as a percentage of total sales	*Total sales*
10%	$10,000 or less
12.5%	10,001 to $15,000
15%	15,001 or more

Write a program to determine the authors' royalties. Use the following data:

Author	*Total sales*
1	$ 14,365
2	6,400
3	200,000
4	16,000
5	15,020

Gateway to effective and efficient programming with FOR-NEXT and subscripted variables

6

It may be refreshing to know that it is not absolutely essential to learn the next two statements, FOR and NEXT. Anything that can be done with these statements can be done using a combination of LET, IF, and GO TO statements. FOR and NEXT statements are extremely convenient, and like so many other conveniences, it would be extremely difficult to get along without them.

FOR AND NEXT

FOR and NEXT statements are used together to create loops in a BASIC program. *The FOR statement is the first statement in the loop, and the NEXT statement is the last statement in the loop.* To give you an example of how these statements can be used, Application 5-4 will be modified to use these statements.

Application 6-1

Application 5-4 calculates average and total sales by using a loop to accumulate the total sales. Now, FOR and NEXT statements will be used to create the same loop. The flowchart is shown in Figure 6-1.

After T is set equal to 0 and M is assigned a value of 7 in the READ statement, the computer enters a loop at the FOR statement in line 30. During the first loop, I is 1; during the second loop, I is 2, and so forth. In each loop, a new value for X is read and added to the total, T. This process continues until the computer cycles 7 times. Then, the computer proceeds as usual and prints the results. As mentioned previously, the NEXT statement is the last statement in the loop.

Program 6-1

```
10 LET T = 0
20 READ M
30 FOR I = 1 TO M
40 READ X
50 LET T = T + X
60 NEXT I
70 PRINT "THE TOTAL IS",T
80 PRINT "THE AVERAGE IS",T/M
90 DATA 7
100 DATA 6,10,8,6
110 DATA 5,15,10.64
9999 END

READY
RUNNH


THE TOTAL IS   60.64
THE AVERAGE IS 8.66286
```

The general form of both statements is given below:

The FOR statement:

line # FOR [index variable] = [expression 1] to [expression 2]

or

line # FOR [index variable] = [expression 1] to [expression 2] STEP [expression 3]

The NEXT statement:

line # NEXT [index variable]

The index variable is first set equal to expression 1, and then the computer loops until the index variable reaches expression 2. The index variable steps or increases by 1 for each loop unless the STEP option is used. When the STEP option is used, the computer increments the index variable by expression 3. Expression 3 can even be *negative:* this causes the index variable to decrease after every cycle.

In the above program, the variable I is used in both the FOR and NEXT statements. If the same variable is not used in both statements, an error message is printed.

FOR and NEXT statements can be used to simplify programs. Moreover, they can be used effectively to incorporate flexibility and efficiency into otherwise long and cumbersome programs. Consider Application 4-5, which calculates depreciation using the double declining balance method for only four years. If you wanted to extend this program to calculate depreciation for 35 years, about 150 BASIC statements would have to be written. And even worse, if you

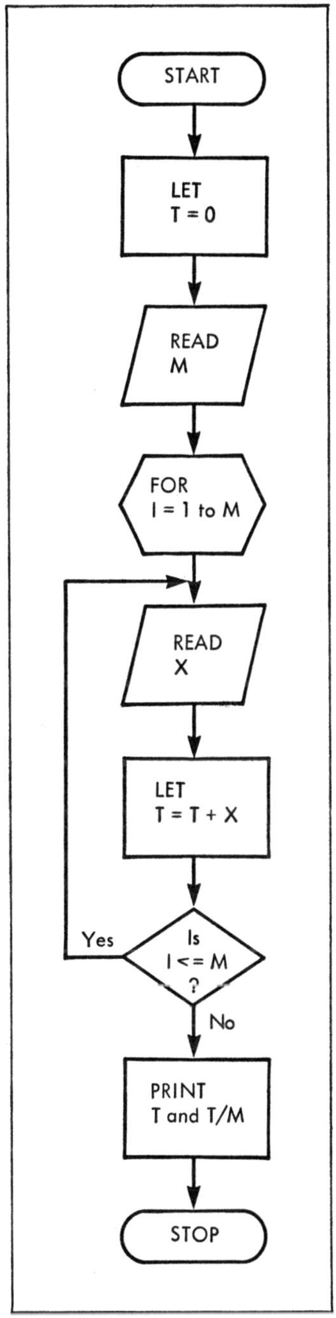

FIGURE 6-1
Flowchart for application 6-1

wanted to change any values, most of the statements would have to be changed. How depressing! But if you use FOR and NEXT statements, you can build flexibility and efficiency into the program. You can run the program hundreds of times using different values and never change one statement.

Application 6-2

W. Lange would like to rewrite the depreciation program using FOR and NEXT statements. All values should remain the same except the asset should be depreciated over 11 years instead of only 4 years.

The power of FOR and NEXT statements is incredible. This program can do much more, but yet it is considerably shorter. Do you

Program 6-2

```
10 REM W. LANGE
20 PRINT "DOUBLE DECLINING BALANCE"
30 PRINT
50 PRINT "PLEASE ENTER V = VALUE, L = USEFUL LIFE AND Y = NO. OF ";
55 PRINT "DEPRECIATION YRS."
58 PRINT "V = "
60 INPUT V
62 PRINT "L = "
64 INPUT L
66 PRINT "Y = "
67 INPUT Y
68 PRINT
69 PRINT "YEAR", "AMOUNT"
70 FOR I = 1 TO Y
80 LET D = (2/L) * V
90 PRINT I, D
100 LET V = V - D
110 NEXT I
120 END

READY
RUNNH

DOUBLE DECLINING BALANCE

PLEASE ENTER V = VALUE, L = USEFUL LIFE AND Y = NO. OF DEPRECIATION YRS.
V =
 ?187000
L =
 ?22
Y =
 ?11

YEAR          AMOUNT
 1             17000
 2             15454.5
 3             14049.6
 4             12772.4
 5             11611.2
 6             10555.7
 7             9596.06
 8             8723.69
 9             7930.63
 10            7209.66
 11            6554.24
```

see how straightforward the loop is? Line 70 starts the loop, line 80 calculates the depeciation, line 90 prints the year (I) and the depreciation (D), line 100 calculates the new value (V), and line 110 sends the computer back to line 70 to calculate and print depreciation for the next year. This is continued until the depreciations for 11 years are printed.

Application 6-3

K. Stearns, who has an account with First Republic Bank, is thinking about placing $1,800 in the regular savings plan at 5¾ percent or the Silver Star plan at 7¼ percent. Although the Silver Star plan has a higher interest rate, withdrawals can be made only four times a year. Program 6-3 calculates the future value of $1,800 after each year for ten years for both plans.

$$F = 1{,}800\left(1 + \frac{I}{12}\right)^{12N}$$

where

F = future value (compounded monthly)
I = annual interest rate
N = number of years

With a handful of BASIC statements, the computer can be commanded to perform hundreds of calculations. Indeed, if you changed line 30 to be: 30 FOR N = 1 TO 1000, this program would calculate and print 2,000 numbers. This shows the real power of FOR and

Program 6-3

```
10 REM K. STEARNS
20 PRINT "YEAR","REGULAR","SILVER STAR"
30 FOR N = 1 TO 10
40 LET R = 1800*(1+.0575/12)**(12*N)
50 LET S = 1800*(1+.0725/12)**(12*N)
60 PRINT N,R,S
70 NEXT N
80 END

READY
RUNNH

YEAR          REGULAR       SILVER STAR
 1             1906.27       1934.92
 2             2018.82       2079.96
 3             2138.01       2235.87
 4             2264.23       2403.47
 5             2397.91       2583.63
 6             2539.49       2777.29
 7             2689.42       2985.47
 8             2848.2        3209.26
 9             3016.35       3449.82
 10            3194.44       3708.41
```

NEXT statements. You can write a short program that will cause the computer to make literally thousands of calculations.

Now suppose K. Stearns wants to expand the above program to calculate the future value from 5¾ percent to 7¼ percent in ½ percent increments and from one to ten years in one-year increments. Of course, you could add several LET statements to calculate the future value at 5¾ percent, 6½ percent, 6¾ percent, and 7¼ percent. Since there are *two variables* incrementing, interest rate and number of years, why don't we use *two loops?* Let the computer do the work.

Application 6-4

K. Stearns would like to calculate the future value of $1,800 for interest rates of 5¾ percent to 7¼ percent in steps of ½ percent for all ten years.

Program 6-4

```
10 REM K. STEARNS
20 PRINT "YEAR"," 5 3/4"," 6 1/4"," 6 3/4"," 7 1/4"
25 PRINT
30 FOR N = 1 TO 10
40 PRINT N,
50 FOR I = .0575 TO .0725 STEP .005
60 PRINT 1800*(1+I/12)**(12*N),
70 NEXT I
80 PRINT
90 NEXT N
100 END

READY
RUNNH
```

YEAR	5 3/4	6 1/4	6 3/4	7 1/4
1	1906.27	1915.78	1925.33	1934.92
2	2018.82	2039.01	2059.39	2079.96
3	2138.01	2170.16	2202.78	2235.87
4	2264.23	2309.75	2356.15	2403.47
5	2397.91	2458.31	2520.21	2583.63
6	2539.49	2616.43	2695.68	2777.29
7	2689.42	2784.73	2883.38	2985.47
8	2848.2	2963.85	3084.14	3209.26
9	3016.35	3154.49	3298.88	3449.82
10	3194.44	3357.39	3528.57	3708.41

Program 6-4 is only two statements larger than the previous program, but it calculates 20 additional future values. Here is how it works. Line 30 sets N = 1 for the first loop, and then N, which is 1, is printed in line 40. See the comma after N in line 40. This causes the next value to be printed in the same line. Lines 50 through 70 are the *inside* loop. This loop prints the future value of $1,800 for the interest rate beginning at 5¾ to 7¼ with a step or increment of 0.005. This inner loop cycles four times, printing all the values on the same line because there is a comma at the end of the PRINT statement in line 60. After the inner loop cycles four times, the computer drops down to line 80. The word PRINT, with nothing after it, causes the computer to print the next value on a new line. Without line 80, the computer would attempt to print *all* values on the same line. At line 90, the computer is directed to start the entire process over again for the second year. This continues until all ten years have been processed.

Perhaps now you are beginning to realize the value of a computer system. Suppose you wanted these calculations for 100 years. This would be 400 numbers. Even with an average hand calculator, you would be pounding calculator keys for hours. It would be so much easier to change the number 10 to100 in line 30. As someone once said, "I love work; I could watch it all day!" Why not relax and watch the computer do the work? It will work for you 24 hours a day without demanding fringe benefits or higher wages.

A flowchart of the Program 6-4 clearly shows the inner and outer loops of this program. The flowchart appears in Figure 6-2.

It is not uncommon to place one loop inside another as long as the loops do not "overlap" or "cross." If you draw lines, as was done in the previous flowchart, connecting the FOR and NEXT statements, you can immediately see whether or not the loops are crossed (see Figure 6-3).

Anytime you employ one or more FOR–NEXT loops, you must be careful not to transfer to the middle of a loop as a result of a GO TO or an IF statement. The *only* way to enter a FOR–NEXT loop is from the top, through the FOR statement. Although an error message will result if you enter a loop by *not* going through the FOR statement, transferring out of the middle of a loop is allowable.

FOR and NEXT statements give programmers the ability to do more with less effort, but this new capability causes new problems. For example, how would you write a program to compute both the average and standard deviation of a series of numbers? The procedure for doing this by hand is given on page 67.

FIGURE 6-2
Flowchart for application 6-4

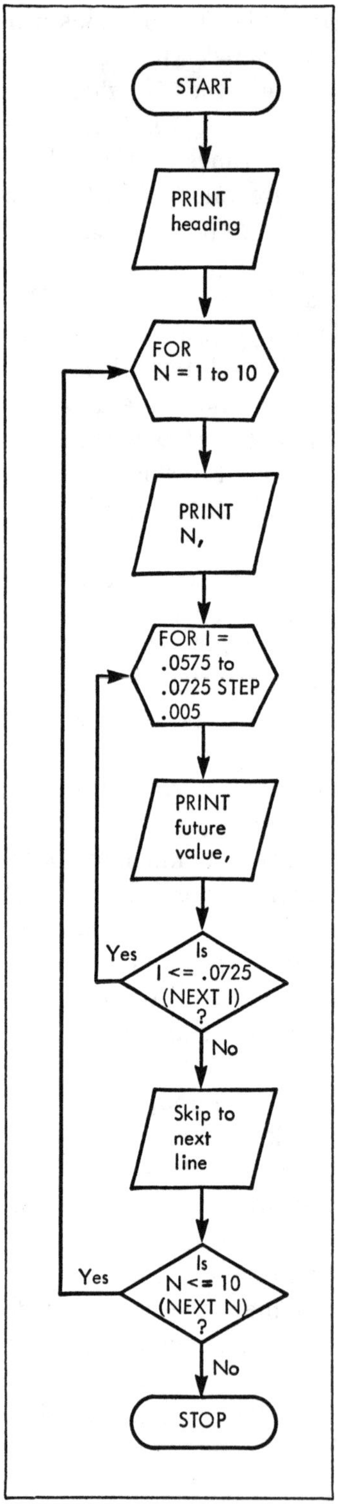

These loops will cause an error message	*These loops are acceptable*
FOR A FOR B NEXT A NEXT B	FOR A FOR B NEXT B NEXT A
FOR I FOR J FOR K NEXT J NEXT K NEXT I	FOR I FOR J NEXT J FOR K NEXT K NEXT I

FIGURE 6-3
Nested FOR–NEXT loops

1. Calculate the average,

$$A = \frac{\Sigma X}{N}$$

where

A = The average
X = The values to be averaged
Σ = The sum of the values
N = The number of values

2. Calculate the standard deviation,

$$S = \sqrt{\frac{\Sigma(X-A)^2}{N-1}}$$

Note: $\Sigma(X-A)^2$ is calculated as follows:

a. subtract the average from each of the values
b. square all the terms of step (a)
c. add or take the sum, Σ, of the results of step (b)

Here is the difficulty in writing the program. In order to calculate the average, you have to read *all* the values. As you recall, each time you read a new X value, the old or previous value is lost. When you attempt to calculate the standard deviation in the program, you have to read *all* the values again, but these values, in DATA statements, have already been used and are lost. Of course, you could repeat all the DATA statements, but there is an easier way to *restore* the data statements to their original condition so the values can be read again.

RESTORE

The RESTORE statement places all the DATA statements in their original state. Thus after a RESTORE statement, you can read all the data again for further processing. The form of the RESTORE statement is:

line # RESTORE

Application 6-5

M. LeBoeuf is concerned about unpaid medical bills for River Road Medical Clinic. The clinic has a minicomputer, and he would like to write a program to calculate the average and standard deviation of the number of days a client takes to pay his or her bill. The program is shown in Program 6-5.

The first half of the program computes the average. Then line 120 restores the DATA statements to their original state. The second half of the program computes the standard deviation. Why is line 125 essential? N was already read in line 40. Would the program work without line 125? No! Without line 125, the computer would read the number 20 in line 900 as the first X value, but 20 is N, the num-

Program 6-5

```
10 REM M. LEBOUF
20 REM AVG. AND STD. OF DAYS TO PAY BILL
30 REM N IS NO. OF CLIENTS
40 READ N
50 REM AVERAGE IS CALCULATED BELOW
55 LET S = 0
60 FOR I = 1 TO N
70 READ X
80 LET S = S + X
90 NEXT I
100 LET A = S/N
110 REM STANDARD DEVIATION CALCULATED BELOW
120 RESTORE
125 READ N
130 LET S = 0
140 FOR I = 1 TO N
150 READ X
160 LET S = S + (X-A)**2
170 NEXT I
180 LET S1 = SQR (S/(N-1))
190 PRINT "THE AVERAGE IS",A
200 PRINT "THE STANDARD DEVIATION IS",S1
900 DATA 20
910 DATA 13,47,61,52,7
920 DATA 16,14,31,55,61
930 DATA 14,104,22,21,19
940 DATA 12,22,26,35,61
9999 END

READY
RUNNH


THE AVERAGE IS 34.65
THE STANDARD DEVIATION IS    24.6518
```

ber of clients, and *not* X, the time it takes a client to pay his or her bill. Although there would be no error messages, the standard deviation would be wrong. This is an example of a logical error.

There is another way, other than a RESTORE statement, to use data more than once in a program. Use a different variable to represent each value. The next section not only shows how to accomplish this task efficiently, but also explains an excellent method of handling a list of numbers or a table of numbers.

SUBSCRIPTED VARIABLES

Subscripted variables are used to represent a list or a table of numbers. If you want to calculate the average and standard deviation of a list of numbers, you could let X_1 be the first number, X_2 the second number, and so forth. A subscripted variable can also be used to represent a table of numbers. In a teacher's grade book, for example, each row could be a student, and each column could be an exam score. Thus $X_{1,2}$ would be the exam score of the first student on the second exam; $X_{3,1}$ would be the third student's first exam score; $X_{6,3}$ would be the sixth student's third exam score. Do you see the pattern? The *first* number is the *row* or student, and the *second* number is the *column* or the exam number.

Subscripted variables can be used as any other variable, but in BASIC they must have the following form:

Variable (expression)—such as X (6)

or

Variable (expression, expression)—such as Y (4, 2)

When you use a subscripted variable, the values are kept in memory while the program is being executed. Consider the following statements:

```
10 FOR I = 1 TO 4
20 READ X(I)
30 NEXT I
40 DATA 8, 4, 7, 2
```

Here is what is stored in memory:

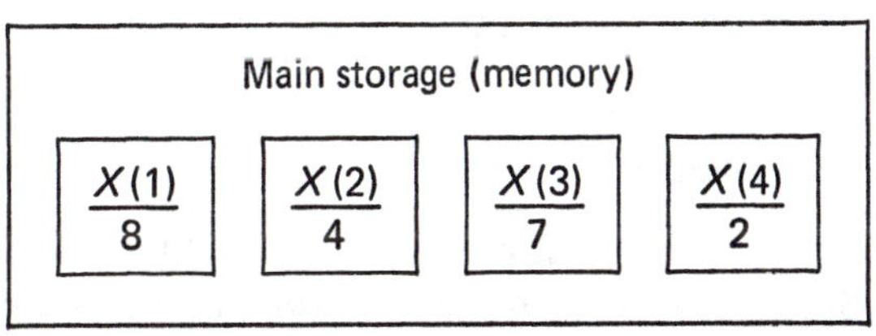

Now consider a table of numbers in the following statements:

```
10 FOR I = 1 TO 2
20 FOR J = 1 TO 3
30 READ Y(I,J)
40 NEXT J
50 NEXT I
60 DATA 2, 9, 4
70 DATA 6, 1, 7
```

Here is what is stored in memory:

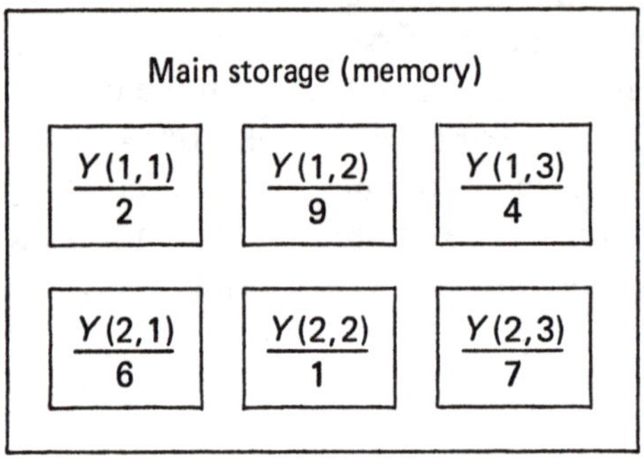

DIMENSION

Any time a subscript in a subscripted variable is greater than ten, you must reserve space in the computer's memory using one or more DIMENSION statements. The form of the DIMENSION statement is below:

```
line # DIM variable (number)
```

or

```
line # DIM variable (number, number)
```

It should be noted that several subscripted variables may appear in one DIMENSION statement. Furthermore, the number must represent the greatest value that the subscript will reach in running the program. Table 6-1 shows some typical DIMENSION statements.

Usually the DIM statement is placed at the beginning of a program. This will be illustrated in the next application.

Application 6-6

The Do-It-Yourself Frame Company, operated and owned by R. Stewart, sells framing kits for paintings and pictures to hobby stores

TABLE 6-1
DIMENSION statements

Proper	Improper	Explanation
10 DIM X(10)	10 DIM X(N)	N should be a number.
5 DIM Y(30,40)	5 DIN Y(30,40)	Misspelling.
15 DIM X(100), A(30,20)	15 DIM X(100), A(20,20	One parenthesis is needed.

across the United States. The company carries 14 different types of frames. Stewart has kept records of units sold and the profit margin for each type of frame. This information is shown in Table 6-2.

Stewart would like to calculate the total profit from last year's sales. Program 6-6 makes the calculations.

Look at line 30. Why are the subscripted variables dimensioned for 20 numbers when only 14 are needed? Stewart knew that more frame types would be added to the inventory in the near future. Thus, the subscripted variables were dimensioned for 20 numbers or frame types to allow for the added items. Thus line 30 will not have to be changed every time a new frame type is added to the product line.

Figure 6-4 contains the flowchart for this program.

As can be seen in Figure 6-4, the program is a combination of several short and easy-to-understand FOR–NEXT loops. The first loop, lines 50, 60, and 70, reads the frame numbers. The second loop reads the number of frames of each type, and the third loop reads

TABLE 6-2
Frame sales for last year

Frame number	Number sold	Profit margin
F(1) → 101	N(1) → 3210	M(1) → .21
F(2) → 102	N(2) → 1040	M(2) → .25
F(3) → 103	N(3) → 87	M(3) → .26
104	2011	.26
. 105	. 4061	. .41
. 106	. 146	. .21
. 107	. 2117	. .21
108	1986	.31
109	2512	.36
110	1116	.22
111	1814	.11
112	3011	.26
113	168	.19
F(14) → 114	N(14) → 2114	M(14) → .11

Program 6-6

```
10 REM TOTAL PROFIT MARGIN
20 REM BY RANDY STEWART
30 DIM F(20), N(20), M(20), P(20)
40 READ N
45 LET T = 0
50 FOR I = 1 TO N
60 READ F(I)
70 NEXT I
80 FOR I = 1 TO N
90 READ N(I)
100 NEXT I
110 FOR I = 1 TO N
120 READ M(I)
130 NEXT I
140 PRINT "FRAME NUMBER","NUMBER SOLD","PROFIT MARGIN","PROFIT"
150 FOR I = 1 TO N
160 LET P(I) = N(I) * M(I)
170 PRINT F(I),N(I),M(I),P(I)
180 LET T = T + P(I)
190 NEXT I
200 PRINT
210 PRINT "TOTAL PROFIT        IS", T
1000 DATA 14
1010 DATA 101,102,103,104,105,106,107
1020 DATA 108,109,110,111,112,113,114
1030 DATA 3210,1040,87,2011,4061,146,2117
1040 DATA 1986,2512,1116,1814,3011,168,2114
1050 DATA .21,.25,.26,.26,.41,.21,.21
1060 DATA .31,.36,.22,.11,.26,.19,.11
9999 END

READY
RUNNH


FRAME NUMBER  NUMBER SOLD   PROFIT MARGIN PROFIT
 101           3210          0.21          674.1
 102           1040          0.25          260
 103           87            0.26          22.62
 104           2011          0.26          522.86
 105           4061          0.41          1665.01
 106           146           0.21          30.66
 107           2117          0.21          444.57
 108           1986          0.31          615.66
 109           2512          0.36          904.32
 110           1116          0.22          245.52
 111           1814          0.11          199.54
 112           3011          0.26          782.86
 113           168           0.19          31.92
 114           2114          0.11          232.54

TOTAL PROFIT        IS       6632.18
```

the profit margin for each frame type. The fourth loop calculates the profit margin for each frame in line 160, and in line 170 the results for each frame are printed. Finally, the total profit is computed in line 180 and printed in line 210.

When subscripted variables are used, the computer retains all the values in the computer's memory, and each step can be done separately. Subscripted variables can be used when a list of numbers is to be processed as in the above program. Subscripted variables can also

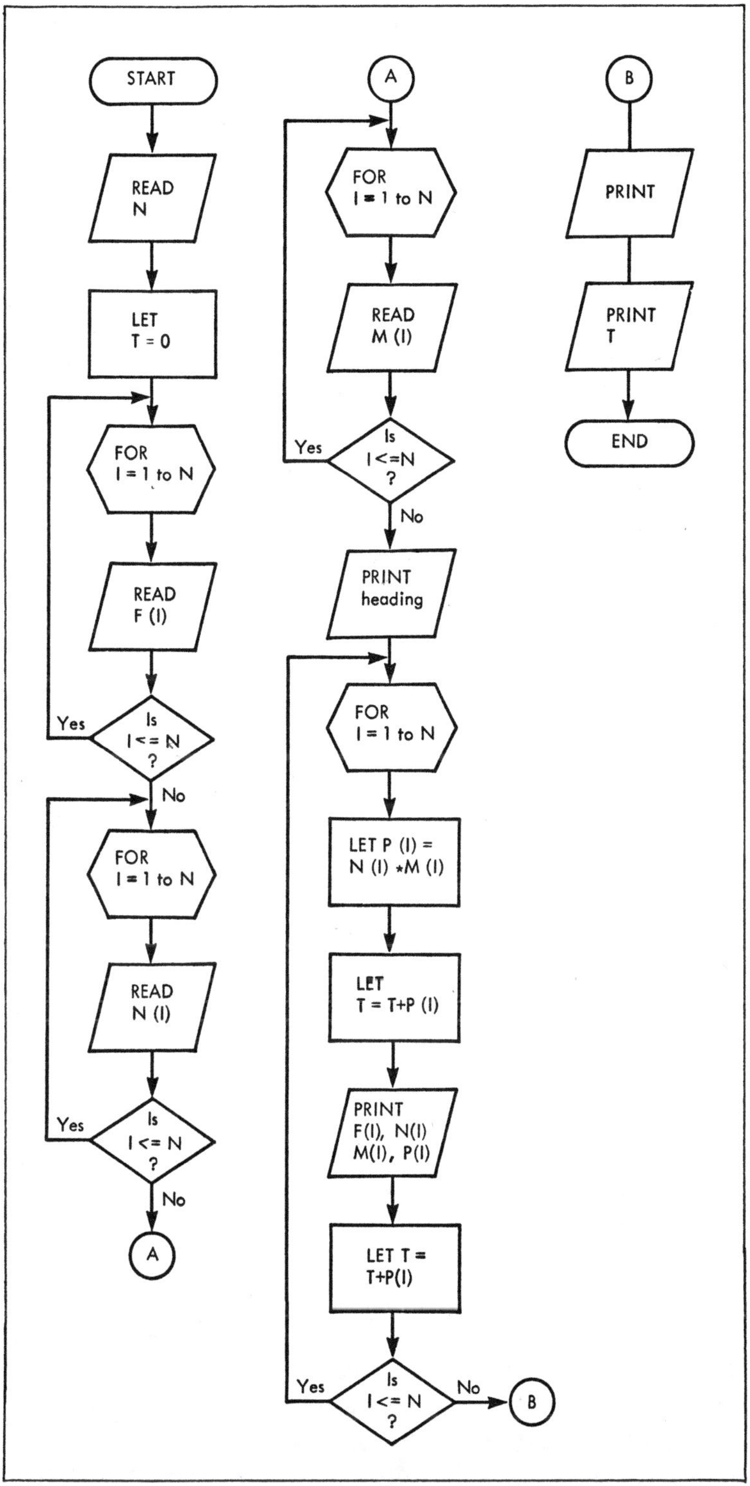

FIGURE 6-4
Flowchart for application 6-6

be used to process a table of numbers. The following application is an example.

Application 6-7

J. Sitlington, a local consultant, has been hired to evaluate a federally funded program at a junior college. Three important questions were administered to students involved in the program. A standard five-point scale was used.

1. How well was the program managed?
2. How well did the program meet your needs?
3. How would you rate the program overall?

Tables 6-3 and 6-4 reveal the results for two years.

TABLE 6-3
Results for the first year (number of responses to each question)

	Question		
Response	*1*	*2*	*3*
1—Poor	21	14	19
2—Fair	36	45	41
3—Average	63	75	70
4—Good	108	88	99
5—Excellent	32	46	41

TABLE 6-4
Results for the second year (number of responses to each question)

	Question		
Response	*1*	*2*	*3*
1—Poor	46	61	52
2—Fair	37	42	44
3—Average	86	80	91
4—Good	51	52	40
5—Excellent	30	36	21

Sitlington now must write a program to calculate the total response for each question for both years. In other words, the two tables must be added to create a third table. See Program 6-7.

Observing what happens in the computer's memory reveals one advantage of using subscripted variables. A large number of values

Program 6-7

```
10 REM J. SITLINGTON
20 REM ANALYSIS OF FEDERAL PROGRAM
30 REM READ TABLE 6.3 AS X(I,J)
40 FOR I = 1 TO 5
50 FOR J = 1 TO 3
60 READ X(I,J)
70 NEXT J
80 NEXT I
90 REM READ TABLE 6.4 AS Y(I,J)
100 FOR I = 1 TO 5
110 FOR J = 1 TO 3
120 READ Y(I,J)
130 NEXT J
140 NEXT I
150 REM CALCULATE AND PRINT TOTAL RESPONSE
160 PRINT "RESPONSE","QUESTION 1","QUESTION 2","QUESTION 3"
170 FOR I = 1 TO 5
180 PRINT I,
190 FOR J = 1 TO 3
200 LET Z(I,J) = X(I,J) + Y(I,J)
210 PRINT Z(I,J),
220 NEXT J
230 PRINT
240 NEXT I
250 REM CALCULATE AND PRINT QUESTION 3 AVERAGE FOR 1ST YEAR
260 LET T = 0
270 LET S = 0
280 FOR I = 1 TO 5
290 LET T = T + Z(I,3)
300 LET X = S + Z(I,3) * I
310 NEXT I
320 PRINT
330 PRINT
340 PRINT "THE AVERAGE RESPONSES FOR QUESTION 3 IS",S/I
1000 REM DATA FROM THE FIRST YEAR
1010 DATA 21,14,19
1020 DATA 36,45,41
1030 DATA 63,75,70
1040 DATA 108,88,99
1050 DATA 32,46,41
1070 REM DATA FROM THE SECOND YEAR
1080 DATA 46,61,52
1090 DATA 37,42,44
1095 DATA 86,80,91
1100 DATA 51,52,40
1120 DATA 30,36,21
9000 END

READY
RUNNH

RESPONSE      QUESTION 1    QUESTION 2    QUESTION 3
 1             67            75            71
 2             73            87            85
 3             149           155           161
 4             159           140           139
 5             62            82            62
```

can be read, processed, and printed in a very efficient manner. Furthermore, analyzing what goes on in the computer's memory can give insights into how the program works. The contents of the computer's memory appear on the next page.

Here is how the program works. In line 40, I is set equal to 1; in

Main storage (memory)

The X(I,J) matrix read in lines 40-80

I	J: 1	2	3
1	21	14	19
2	36	45	41
3	63	75	70
4	108	88	99
5	32	46	41

The Y(I,J) matrix read in lines 100-140

I	J: 1	2	3
1	46	61	52
2	37	42	44
3	86	80	91
4	51	52	40
5	30	36	21

The Z(I,J) matrix calculated and printed in lines 160-240

I	J: 1	2	3
1	67	75	71
2	73	87	85
3	149	155	161
4	159	140	139
5	62	82	62

line 50, J is set equal to 1; and in line 60, X(1,1) is read from the first data statement and assigned a value of 21. Then J becomes 2, and X(1,2) becomes 14. Then X(1,3) becomes 19. Since J only goes from 1 to 3, the computer drops down to the NEXT I statement in line 80, and I becomes 2. J starts at 1, and X(2,1) is set equal to 36. Do you see the pattern? These statements read the data by rows. Look at the X(I,J) matrix stored in memory. What is X(2,2)? It is 45, the number in the second row and second column of the X(I,J) matrix. What is X(4,3)? It is read from the data as 99. It is the number in the fourth row and third column of the matrix. The two FOR–NEXT loops cause the data to be read in a systematic fashion. Could you use fewer DATA statements? Yes. As long as the data are in the correct order, you can use as many or as few DATA statements as you wish.

Next, the Y(I, J) matrix of numbers is read. The procedure is identical to the one described above for the X(I, J) matrix. For example, what is Y(4,1)? It is 51, the number in the fourth row and the first column. After all 15 numbers are read and stored as Y(I, J) values, the computer calculates and prints the Z(I, J) matrix. Line 160 prints a heading. Line 180 prints I. Line 200 calculates Z(I, J), and line 210 prints the value. The commas at the end of lines 180 and 210 cause all the values to be printed on the same line. PRINT in line 230 skips to the next line. Thus the second row of values is printed on the second line. (Of course, these statements were carefully written to accomplish this.) Line 240, which is NEXT I, causes the computer to go back to line 170 to add the appropriate numbers for every row and column.

SUMMARY

FOR–NEXT loops and subscripted variables are convenient. Think about having to write the last few programs without these statements. It is possible, but it will drive you to the edge of insanity. These statements are also very powerful. They can force a computer to make thousands of calculations from a handful of BASIC statements. It would take you hours of sweating and swearing to make the same calculations by hand. The computer is obedient and never tiring, and if you know how to command and control it, you can save yourself the agony of performing mundane data processing tasks in other courses, at school, and at work.

You now know about 12 BASIC statements, but more important, you have seen how these statements can be used to construct realistic computer programs. Computers are being successfully used in organizations such as police departments, hospitals, and city governments, in addition to businesses. Many of the computer programs used in these organizations can be written using the BASIC statements covered in Chapters 3 through 6.

QUESTIONS

6-1. What is the primary purpose of FOR–NEXT statements?

6-2. What are the general forms of the FOR and NEXT statements?

6-3. What does the RESTORE statement accomplish?

6-4. Under what circumstances are subscripted variables useful in BASIC programs?

6-5. What is the general form of a subscripted variable with one subscript? With two subscripts?

6-6. The following table contains the sales in millions of dollars for ten products in four divisions:

Product	Division 1	2	3	4
1	5.6	2.4	4.4	6.7
2	3.5	5.0	6.1	1.2
3	5.3	2.2	8.2	9.0
4	2.3	5.4	3.4	6.7
5	3.5	6.6	5.6	3.4
6	3.3	5.4	2.3	7.6
7	4.5	6.1	3.3	4.5
8	2.3	4.5	6.1	5.0
9	5.5	4.7	7.1	5.6
10	3.3	1.2	1.2	3.1

Write a program to determine the total sales for each division.

6-7. Using the Bernoulli process it is possible to determine the probability of obtaining a given number of successes out of a given number of trials if there are only two possible outcomes and the probability of a success remains the same. The formula is below.

$$\text{Probability} = \frac{N!}{R!(N-R)!} P^{R}(1-P)^{N-R}$$

where

N! is the factorial of the number of trials;
R! is the factorial of the number of successes;
P is the probability of one success;
R is the number of successes;
N is the number of trials;
(N−R)! is the factorial of the number of failures.

Write a program to compute the probability of obtaining R successes out of N trials when the probability of one success is P. Use 5, 8, and 0.3 for R, N, and P to test your program.

7 Some additional features of BASIC including string variables, PRINT USING, TAB, and RND

STRING VARIABLES AND CONSTANTS

In Chapters 2 through 6, you studied how to process numbers. In many computer applications, this is not sufficient. How would you like to get a check from your employer with your employee number instead of your name? In addition to numbers, most organizations must also process names or strings of characters. To accomplish this, computers must have the ability to process a name or any other string of characters.

In order to input, process, and output names or any other character strings, the concepts of BASIC numbers and variables must be expanded. A string constant *is any string of characters enclosed within quotation marks.* In some systems, a string constant in a DATA statement does not require quotation marks. A string variable, *which is used to represent a string constant, is constructed by adding a dollar sign ($) at the end of the variable name.* Table 7-1 gives examples of string constants and variables and reveals the BASIC statements that can handle strings.

As seen below, string constants can be used in DATA, LET, IF, and PRINT statements. String variables can be used in READ, INPUT, LET, IF, PRINT, and DIM statements. In Example 1, the name, "WU, S.", hours, H, and rate, R, are read in line 10. Line 20 prints the name and gross pay. Example 2 reveals the use of IF and LET statements. Line 30 assigns "NO" to X1$. In line 40, X1$ is *not* equal to "YES" and the computer drops down to line 50, where B$ is set equal to "AUGUST". Line 60 directs the computer to GO TO 110. The use of *subscripted string variables* is illustrated in Example 3, which computes gross pay for 20 employees. Note the subscripted string variables in lines 20, 50, and 90. Lines 40, 50, and

TABLE 7-1
String constants and variables

	Example statements (partial programs)	*Strings used in the Examples*
1.	10 READ A$, H, R	A$
	20 PRINT A$, H*R	A$
	30 DATA "WU, S.", 40, 4	WU, S.
2.	30 READ X1$	X1$
	40 IF X1$ = "YES", THEN 60	YES, X1$
	50 LET B$ = "AUGUST"	B$, AUGUST
	60 GO TO 110	
	70 LET B$ = "SEPTEMBER"	SEPTEMBER, B$
	100 DATA "NO"	NO
3.	20 DIM N$(20), R1(20), H1(20)	N$(20)
	30 PRINT "ENTER NAME, RATE, AND HOURS"	(These are messages, not string constants.)
	40 FOR I = 1 TO 20	N$(1), N$(2)...N$(20)
	50 INPUT N$(I), R1(I), H1(I)	
	60 NEXT I	
	70 PRINT "NAME", "GROSS"	
	80 FOR I = 1 TO 20	
	90 PRINT N$(I), R1(I)*H1(I)	N$(1), N$(2)...N$(20)
	100 NEXT I	

60 INPUT the employee name, pay rate, and hours worked in the previous week. The loop, consisting of lines 80, 90, and 100, prints the employee name and gross pay.

The example statements above could be placed in larger programs to process names or character strings as well as numbers. Of course, it would now be possible to modify many of the programs in Chapters 2 through 6 to replace employee numbers with names. Programs can now be made more conversational. Consider the following application.

Application 7-1

Harry L. Legan has been hired to write a conversational program to help managers decide how many units of a particular item to order. In school Harry learned that the following equation gives the number of units to be ordered to minimize total inventory costs for certain types of inventory problems:

$$Q = \sqrt{\frac{2DC1}{C2}}$$

where

D = The annual demand;
C1 = The cost to place an order;
C2 = The cost of carrying one unit for one year (storage costs, opportunity cost, and so on).

Harry's program is shown in Program 7-1.

As can be seen in Application 7-1, computer programs can be as conversational as desired. One disadvantage is the increased program length. The program in Application 7-1 could be written using only a handful of statements if the INPUT and related PRINT statements were removed.

PRINT USING

Other programming languages require you to completely specify where every number and name is to be printed. With BASIC, you have a choice. You can let the computer format output automatically, or you can employ the PRINT USING statement. The form of the PRINT USING statement appears below:

```
line #1 PRINT USING line #2 [a list of expressions]
line #2 : [a string of characters]¹
```

Here are some typical applications.

Application 7-2

Merkel, Leech, Price, Bull, and Schmidt, a local stock and bond firm, needs a program to calculate before-tax profit or loss for its clients. Program 7-2 assumes the total commission is 3 percent of the selling price.

Do you see how easy it is to employ PRINT USING statements? *Each PRINT USING statement refers to another line number where the format or layout of the output is completely described.* The PRINT USING statements in lines 22, 24, and 30 cause the information on lines 1000, 1005, and 1010 to be printed exactly as you see it. These lines cause the computer to print the heading you see on the computer output. The PRINT USING statements in line 100, which is inside the FOR–NEXT loop, prints the stock name, number of shares, purchase price, selling price, commission, and net profit

[1] In some computer systems, FMT replaces the colon.

Program 7-1

```
10 PRINT "HI; WHAT IS YOUR FIRST NAME?"
20 INPUT F$
30 PRINT "WHAT IS YOUR LAST NAME?"
40 INPUT L$
50 PRINT "WHAT IS YOUR TITLE? (MR.,MS.,DR.,ETC.)"
60 INPUT T$
70 PRINT "CAN I CALL YOU BY YOUR FIRST NAME?"
80 PRINT "(YES OR NO)"
90 INPUT A$
100 IF A$ = "NO",THEN 130
110 LET C$ = F$
120 GO TO 140
130 LET C$ = " "
140 PRINT C$;" WOULD YOU LIKE INFORMATION?"
150 INPUT I$
160 IF I$ = "NO",THEN 220
170 PRINT "THIS PROGRAM COMPUTES THE ";
180 PRINT "NUMBER OF UNITS TO ORDER."
190 PRINT "D IS ANNUAL DEMAND"
200 PRINT "C1 IS ORDERING COST"
210 PRINT "C2 IS CARRYING COST"
220 PRINT
230 PRINT "WHAT IS THE NAME OF THE ";
240 PRINT "INVENTORY ITEM?"
250 INPUT N$
260 PRINT "ENTER D, C1, C2"
270 INPUT D,C1,C2
280 LET Q = SQR(2 * D * C1 / C2)
290 PRINT "THIS REPORT WAS PREPARED FOR ";
300 PRINT T$;" ";F$;" ";L$
310 PRINT Q;" IS THE OPTIMAL ORDER QUANTITY ";
320 PRINT "FOR ";N$
330 PRINT
340 PRINT C$;" WOULD YOU LIKE TO PROCESS";
350 PRINT " ANOTHER INVENTORY PRODUCT"
360 INPUT A$
370 IF A$ = "YES",THEN 230
380 PRINT "GOOD BYE ";C$
390 END

READY
RUNNH

HI; WHAT IS YOUR FIRST NAME?
 ?TONY
WHAT IS YOUR LAST NAME?
 ?BILL
WHAT IS YOUR TITLE? (MR.,MS.,DR.,ETC.)
 ?MR.
CAN I CALL YOU BY YOUR FIRST NAME?
(YES OR NO)
 ?YES
TONY WOULD YOU LIKE INFORMATION?
 ?YES
THIS PROGRAM COMPUTES THE NUMBER OF UNITS TO ORDER.
D IS ANNUAL DEMAND
C1 IS ORDERING COST
C2 IS CARRYING COST

WHAT IS THE NAME OF THE INVENTORY ITEM?
 ?1440 HOUSING
ENTER D, C1, C2
 ?1000,4,.5
THIS REPORT WAS PREPARED FOR MR. TONY BILL
 126.491  IS THE OPTIMAL ORDER QUANTITY FOR 1440 HOUSING

TONY WOULD YOU LIKE TO PROCESS ANOTHER INVENTORY PRODUCT
 ?NO
GOOD BYE TONY
```

Program 7-2

```
10 REM READ NUMBER OF TRANSACTIONS
20 READ N
22 PRINT USING 1000," "
24 PRINT USING 1005," "
30 PRINT USING 1010," "
40 FOR I = 1 TO N
50 REM READ STOCK, SHARES, PURCHASE
60 REM AND SELLING PRICE
70 READ S$,S1,P,S2
80 LET C = S1 * S2 * .03
90 LET T = S1 * (S2 - P) - C
100 PRINT USING 1020,S$,S1,P,S2,C,T
110 LET S = S + T
120 NEXT I
130 PRINT USING 1010," "
140 PRINT USING 1030,S
1000:                      PURCHASE    SELLING      SALES       PROFIT
1005: STOCK     SHARES       PRICE       PRICE     COMISSION     (LOSS)
1010:-----------------------------------------------------------------------
1020:  ####      ###,###  $#,###.##  $#,###.##    $#,###.##   ($###,###.##)
1030:                                                TOTAL      ($###,###.##)
9000 DATA 4
9010 DATA AKJ,100,134.75,120.25
9020 DATA BRI,15,65.25,71.50
9030 DATA HAL,1400,106.00,95.25
9040 DATA CCX,425,98.75,106.25
9050 END

READY
RUNNH


                      PURCHASE    SELLING      SALES        PROFIT
STOCK     SHARES        PRICE       PRICE     COMISSION     (LOSS)
-------------------------------------------------------------------
 AKJ        100      $ 134.75   $ 120.25   $  360.75  ($ -1,810.75)
 BRI         15      $  65.25   $  71.50   $   32.18   $      61.58
 HAL      1,400      $ 106.00   $  95.25   $4,000.50  ($-19,050.50)
 CCX        425      $  98.75   $ 106.25   $1,354.69   $  1,832.81
-------------------------------------------------------------------
                                             TOTAL     ($-18,966.86)
```

according to line 1020. Carefully study line 1020. It has many important features. #### is the first character string.[2] It allows four positions for the stock name, S$, to be abbreviated. ###,### reserves space for S1, the number of shares. Note the comma, which also appears in the output. For P, S2, C, and T, the final four items to be printed, a dollar sign and a decimal point appear in line 1020 and in the output. Do you see the right and left parentheses in lines 1020 and 1030? Here is what happens. If the number is negative, then the number that is printed will be enclosed in parentheses.[3] This is standard practice for most financial and accounting statements. Table 7-2 reveals some of these concepts.

[2] Some PRINT USING statements or some computers may use 'CCC, 'RRRR, 'LLLL, or 'EEEE at the end of the line.

[3] This feature does not work on all computer systems.

TABLE 7-2
A summary of PRINT USING features

Character	Example	Meaning
#	#####	Five spaces have been reserved for a name or number.
.	###.##	A decimal point will be printed with three positions before it and two positions after it. 486.3218 would be printed as 486.32.
$	$##.##	A dollar sign will be printed. 6.481 would be printed as $ 6.48.
*	$*####.##	An asterisk will be printed to fill any gaps. 6.481 would be printed as $****6.48.
( )	($###.##)	If the number is negative, it is enclosed in parentheses. –460.26 becomes ($460.26). 361.26, however, would be printed as $361.26.*

*This does not work on some systems.

Don't forget to allow enough positions for the largest number or character string. If not enough positions are provided, there will be an error message, or the computer will delete some of the significant digits. For example, printing 384.41 using ##.## will result in either an error message or the printing of the number 84.41, depending on your computer. Regardless of what your computer system does, this problem should be avoided.

TAB

Another very useful feature of BASIC is TAB. The TAB function, which may appear in any PRINT statement, has the following form:

TAB (Expression)

The TAB function in BASIC is like the tab on a typewriter. First, the expression is evaluated and any numbers to the right of the decimal point are eliminated. For example, 46.31 becomes 46. *Then the computer proceeds to that column.* In this case, the computer goes to column 46. As indicated in Program 7-3 *the computer will start printing in the next column.*

Note: TAB(5); "*" causes an asterisk to be printed in column 6.

Program 7-3

```
10 PRINT "1234567890"
20 PRINT TAB(5);"*"
30 END

READY
RUNNH


1234567890
     *
```

The semicolon (;) insures that the asterisk is printed in the next column. Most TAB functions should be followed with a semicolon.

TAB is very useful in spacing output, but it can also be used to draw graphs, to plot curves, and to produce valuable graphic displays of information.

Application 7-3

Ms. Juhn, a young executive with a bright future, is concerned about the large sums of cash her company keeps in a checking account. Although she has mentioned this to the president and owner several times, he is never convinced. She told him a week ago that $10,000 in a savings account would be worth the following:

$$\text{Value} = 10{,}000\,(I + 1)^{N}$$

where

I = interest rate;
N = number of years.

Using the above equation, Ms. Juhn constructed Table 7-3 using a 5 percent interest rate for 23 years.

Unfortunately, the president was never very good with numbers or tables. Therefore, Ms. Juhn decided to write a computer program to draw a graph of the future value of $10,000 as a function of time. Her program is shown in Program 7-4.

There are two FOR–NEXT loops in the Program 7-4. The first loop reads V$(I), the future value, and N(I), the number of years.

TABLE 7-3
The value of $10,000 invested in a savings account

Number of years at 5 percent	*Value*
Today	$10,000
4	$12,000
7	$14,000
10	$16,000
12	$18,000
14	$20,000
16	$22,000
18	$24,000
20	$26,000
22	$28,000
23	$30,000

Program 7-4

```
10 REM MS. M. JUHN
20 REM GRAPH OF FUTURE VALUES
50 DIM V$(20),N(20)
60 REM V$ IS VALUE, N IS NUMBER OF YEARS
70 REM AT 5 PERCENT
80 FOR I = 1 TO 11
90 READ V$(I),N(I)
100 NEXT I
110 REM THE FOLLOWING STATEMENTS
120 REM DRAW THE GRAPH
130 PRINT "FUTURE VALUES OF $10,000"
140 PRINT "INTEREST IS 5 PERCENT"
150 PRINT
160 PRINT
170 PRINT "DOLLARS             YEARS"
180 PRINT
190 PRINT USING 220," "
200 PRINT USING 210," "
210:         +++++++++++++++++++++++++++++++
220:         0         10        20        30
230 FOR I = 11 TO 1 STEP -1
240 PRINT V$(I);"+";TAB(9+N(I));"*"
250 NEXT I
260 PRINT USING 210," "
270 PRINT USING 220," "
275 PRINT
280 PRINT "                    (EACH + IS ONE YEAR)"
1000 DATA "$10,000",0
1010 DATA "$12,000",4
1020 DATA "$14,000",7
1030 DATA "$16,000",10
1040 DATA "$18,000",12
1050 DATA "$20,000",14
1060 DATA "$22,000",16
1070 DATA "$24,000",18
1080 DATA "$26,000",20
1090 DATA "$28,000",22
1100 DATA "$30,000",23
9999 END

READY
RUNNH



FUTURE VALUES OF $10,000
INTEREST IS 5 PERCENT


DOLLARS             YEARS

          0         10        20        30
          +++++++++++++++++++++++++++++++
$30,000+                         *
$28,000+                        *
$26,000+                      *
$24,000+                    *
$22,000+                  *
$20,000+                *
$18,000+              *
$16,000+            *
$14,000+         *
$12,000+      *
$10,000+  *
          +++++++++++++++++++++++++++++++
          0         10        20        30

                    (EACH + IS ONE YEAR)
```

The second loop, lines 230, 240, and 250, is the key to the program. It constructs the graph by printing asterisks in the appropriate places. This is done by TAB(9+N(I)); "*" in line 240. The 9 is needed to skip over the dollar values such as $30,000+. N(I) is needed to skip over the correct number of years. This allows each asterisk to be printed in the correct position.

RANDOM NUMBERS

RND, the random number function, is a built-in feature of BASIC just like SQR or ABS, previously discussed. It generates a number between 0 and 1 at random. Thus the chance that any number, such as 0.36014271 or 0.77401569, will be generated is the same for any number between 0 and 1. The general form of the RND function is:

RND (expression)

Now, consider Program 7-5.

Program 7-5

```
READY
10 RANDOMIZE
20 PRINT RND(1),RND(1),RND(1)
30 END
RUNNH

 0.815207       0.854793       0.477338
```

As seen below, RND(1) produces different random numbers. It should be noted that any number, variable, or expression could replace the number 1 in line 20. Note RANDOMIZE in line 10. Without line 10, some computers would print the same three random numbers each time the program is run. Some computers require RND(−1) to insure different numbers for each run. If you are not sure whether RANDOMIZE, RND(−1), or nothing is needed, ask your instructor or simply experiment with your computer system.

As previously mentioned, RND(1) generates a number between 0 and 1. You may be wondering why we would ever need to generate a bunch of numbers between 0 and 1 at random. Actually, there are many applications that require the use of random numbers. Indeed, almost every statistics book has a table of random numbers generated by a computer. Below is a typical application of the RND function.

Application 7-4

Almost every sampling plan requires the use of random numbers. Tax returns may be inspected at random, the winner of a state lottery may be selected at random, a questionnaire may be administered to a random sample of home owners, or a random sample of incoming products may be inspected for possible defects.

The purpose of this application is to generate a random sample. Assume that a lot of 1,000 fuel pumps used in automobiles is manufactured by a company. Since it would be too expensive to test every fuel pump, the car manufacturing company that buys the pumps has established a sampling plan. It will take a *random* sample of 25 pumps. If more than five pumps are defective, the entire lot is rejected. Program 7-6 generates a random sample of 25 pumps. Each pump is assigned a number from 1 to 1,000.

Program 7-6

```
10 PRINT "BELOW IS A LIST OF PUMPS (BY NUMBER)."
20 PRINT "EACH PUMP LISTED SHOULD BE INSPECTED"
30 PRINT
40 RANDOMIZE
50 FOR I = 1 TO 25
60 PRINT INT (1000*RND(1)+1),
70 NEXT I
80 END

READY
RUNNH


BELOW IS A LIST OF PUMPS (BY NUMBER).
EACH PUMP LISTED SHOULD BE INSPECTED

 857           641           380           464           258
 885           207           320           899           265
 671           578           784           472           990
 476           48            142           567           260
 519           131           43            307           661
```

Statement 60 needs an explanation. RND (any number) generates a number between 0 and 1 but not including 0 and 1. Thus 0.00000001 is the lowest possible number and 0.99999999 is the highest possible number. 1000*RND(1) + 1 generates a random number that can range from 1000*.00000001 + 1 to 1000*.999999999 + 1 or simply 1.00001 to 1000.9999. When the computer takes the integer, INT, of these numbers, any number from and including 1 to 1000 can be generated. Going through this process can be confusing and bothersome. How would you generate random numbers from a lower value to an upper value using the RND function? In general, here is how it is done.

L is the lower value; U is the upper value. The expression

INT((U – L + 1)*RND(1) + L)

generates a random number from L to U.

Table 7-4 contains several examples starting with L and U from Application 7-4.

RND can be used to generate random numbers for a sampling plan like the one discussed in Application 7-4. RND has many other interesting and useful applications. With RND, you can program the computer to act like or *simulate* the intervals at which people arrive at a bank or at the emergency room of a hospital. You can program a computer to act like the stock market, a supermarket, or a lumber mill. Life is filled with uncertainties. Many events happen by chance or at random. RND can be used to act like or simulate these events. But what is the practical value of making a computer act like a random event such as the arrival of a patient at the emergency room of a hospital? If you have decided to cut the emergency room staff, it would be much better to try your decision on the computer first instead of trying your decision in the hospital where lives may be lost as a result. Some decisions cannot be made using profit or loss as the criterion.

TABLE 7-4
Generating random numbers

L (*lower value*)	*U* (*upper value*)	*INT((U – L + 1) * RND(1) + L)* (*random number from L to H*)
1	1000	INT((1000 – 1 + 1) * RND(1) + 1) or INT(1000 * RND(1) + 1)
1 minute	60 minutes	INT((60 – 1 + 1) * RND(1) + 1) or INT(60 * RND(1) + 1)
50	100	INT((100 – 50 + 1) * RND(1) + 50) or INT(51 * RND(1) + 50)

SUMMARY

New ways of printing results have been explored in this chapter. In addition, you have learned how to cause the computer to branch to one of many possible branches using just one simple statement. You have also seen how a computer can be instructed to simulate random events and how this information can be used in decision making. In the next chapter, you will learn how to define your own functions.

QUESTIONS

7-1. What will the following statements cause the computer to do?

a. 10 LET X$ = "NO"

b. 40 READ Y$,A,B$
100 DATA "ONE", 6, "TWO"

c. 10 IF X$ = "NO", THEN 60

d. 10 PRINT "1111111111"
20 PRINT TAB (9/4); 1

e. 10 PRINT USING 35, 100
35 : VALUE IS ###

7-2. Modify Program 5-3 to use *student name* instead of student number. Use the following names:

Student	*Student name*	*Student*	*Student name*
1	Anderson	6	Humphrey
2	Cohen	7	Dyer
3	Bechtold	8	Soloman
4	Anthony	9	Malley
5	Keim	10	King

7-3. Ken Ramsing makes one inspection of his machine shop in the morning (8-12) and one inspection in the afternoon (1-5). To keep the employees alert and honest, Ken has decided to pick the inspection times at random. Write a program to accomplish this. The output should be as follows (of course, your inspection times will be different each time you run your program):

```
  MORNING INSPECTION: 9:12
AFTERNOON INSPECTION: 4:26
```

7-4. Raffle tickets were sold for $1 each to raise funds for the Business Students Association (BSA). Ticket numbers range from 101 through 953. Write a program that will randomly select the winner, who will win a ten-speed bike, by generating one number from 101 through 953 at random.

Using subroutines and user-defined functions with DEF and GO SUB

8

In Chapter 3 you observed how easy it is to use the built-in mathematical functions. SQR is used for square root, ABS calculates the absolute value, INT produces the integer portion of any number, and so forth. But what do you do when the same calculation is repeated several times, but the necessary mathematical function does not exist? The answer is to build or *define* your own function. This can be accomplished by using the DEF statement.

DEF is used to define your own function in BASIC. DEF statements have the following form: **DEF**

```
line # DEF FN [any letter] ([any variable]) = [Expression]
```

As many as 26 functions can be defined in a program—one function for each letter in the alphabet. Thus you may use FNA, FNB, or any function up to FNZ. The variable in a DEF statement is a "dummy" variable; it is used to indicate what calculations are to be made. Actually any variable can be used. Table 8-1 reveals the DEF statement in action.

As seen in the table examples, the DEF statement uses a "dummy" variable to instruct the computer what calculations are to be made. Then in other statements the "dummy" variable is replaced with a number or a variable, and the appropriate calculations are made.

TABLE 8-1
Examples of the DEF statement

Example	*Explanation*
10 DEF FNA(X) = (1 + X)**2	The function is defined.
20 LET Z = FNA(2)	Z is 9; (1 + 2)**2 is 9.
30 LET P = FNA(4)	P is 25; (1 + 4)**2 is 25.
40 DEF FNY(N) = (1+.06)↑N	The function is defined.
50 LET Y1 = FNY(1)	Y1 is 1.06; (1 + .06) ↑ 1 is 1.06.
60 LET Y2 = FNY(2)	Y2 is 1.1236; (1 + .06) ↑ 2 is 1.1236.
70 LET Y3 = FNY(3)	Y3 is 1.191016; (1+.06)↑3 is 1.191016.
25 DEF FNB(X) = X↑2	FNB is defined.
35 DEF FNC(X) = FNB(X)−X	FNC is defined.
45 LET V1 = FNB(3)	V1 is 9; 3↑2 is 9.
55 LET V2 = FNC(3)	V2 is 6; 3↑2−3 is 6.

Application 8-1

Family Finance Corporation (FFC) offers a wide range of services to its clients. Since it makes loans to individuals or families, it is in the process of writing several computer programs to calculate monthly payments. To show FFC's clients the effect of interest rates on monthly payments, Mr. Albert Baccon would like to write a short program, using \$10,000 as the amount of the loan, for five years with these interest rates: 9, 11, 13, and 15 percent.

The appropriate equation is

$$P = \frac{10{,}000\left(\frac{I}{12}\right)\left(1 + \frac{I}{12}\right)^{(12\times 5)}}{\left(1 + \left(\frac{I}{12}\right)\right)^{(12\times 5)} - 1},$$

where

P = Monthly payment;
I = Annual interest rate.

Since the above equation is complex and because it is to be used several times in the short program as well as in other programs to be written later, it should be expressed in a DEF statement. See Program 8-1.

The advantage of the above DEF statement is apparent. Can you imagine trying to repeat that complex expression four times in one PRINT statement? It would be almost impossible. Furthermore, it would be extremely difficult to insert that complex expression four times in the same PRINT statement without making any mistakes.

Program 8-1

```
10 REM - MONTHLY REPORT
20 DEF FNM(I) = (10000*(I/12)*(1+I/12)**(12*5))/((1+I/12)**(12*5)-1)
30 PRINT "INTEREST-","    9%","    11%","    13%","    15%"
35 PRINT
40 PRINT "PAYMENT-",FNM(.09),FNM(.11),FNM(.13),FNM(.15)
50 END

READY
RUNNH


INTEREST-       9%             11%            13%            15%

PAYMENT-      207.584        217.424        227.531        237.899
```

With DEF, these problems are eliminated, and the same function, FNM(I), can be used in other programs.

Mr. Baccon would also like to write a program that changes the amount of the loan and the number of years the loan is outstanding to show potential clients how their monthly payment would change as a function of amount and number of years. Can you use the DEF statement in line 20 for this new program? The answer is NO! The DEF statement permits only one variable such as I. This is one of the major disadvantages of the DEF statement. As you have probably guessed, there is a way of avoiding this problem.

GO SUB–RETURN

A *SUB*routine is used for the same reasons as the DEF statement. When one or more complex calculations are performed several times in one or more programs, a subroutine should be considered. *A subroutine is a mini-program that is placed inside a normal program. The GO SUB statement sends the computer to the subroutine, and the RETURN statement sends the computer back to where it left off in the main program.* The form of these two statements is below:

line # GO SUB line #
line # RETURN

Application 8-2

Family Finance Corporation has decided to write a subroutine that calculates monthly payments. This subroutine is to be used in several programs, but Mr. Baccon would like a short program that will INPUT the amount, number of years, and interest rate. The program is then to go to the subroutine to calculate the monthly payments. Finally, the main program should print the results. See Program 8-2.

Program 8-2

```
10 REM - MAIN PROGRAM AND SUBROUTINE
20 PRINT "ENTER AMOUNT, THE NUMBER OF YEARS,";
30 PRINT " AND INTEREST RATE AS A DECIMAL"
40 INPUT A,N,I
50 GO SUB 1000
60 PRINT "MONTHLY PAYMENT IS",M
70 PRINT
80 PRINT "WOULD YOU LIKE TO MAKE ANOTHER CALCULATION?"
90 PRINT "YES OR NO";
100 INPUT X$
110 IF X$ = "YES" THEN 20
120 STOP
1000 REM SUBROUTINE
1010 LET M = (A*I/12*(1+I/12)**(12*N))/((1+I/12)**(12*N)-1)
1020 RETURN
9999 END

READY
RUNNH


ENTER AMOUNT, THE NUMBER OF YEARS, AND INTEREST RATE AS A DECIMAL
 ?10000,10,.09
MONTHLY PAYMENT IS           126.676

WOULD YOU LIKE TO MAKE ANOTHER CALCULATION?
YES OR NO ?NO
```

You may have noticed the STOP statement in the main program. The STOP statement has the following general form:

line # STOP

The STOP statement may appear anywhere in the program, and there can be as many STOP statements in a program as you want. When the computer encounters the STOP statement, it terminates the execution of the program. If you use the STOP statement, do not forget to place the END statement at the end of the program. As you recall, the last statement in every program must be the END statement.

It is not uncommon to have programs that have more than 1,000 statements. Every day, data processing departments are asked to develop large programs in a relatively short time. But how is this accomplished? Usually, the data processing department will have several programmers writing one computer program. This, however, can cause coordination problems. How can several programmers work on the same program when the statements written by one programmer may be in conflict with the statements written by another programmer? An excellent way of avoiding coordination problems, when several programmers are involved in writing the same program, is to use subroutines.

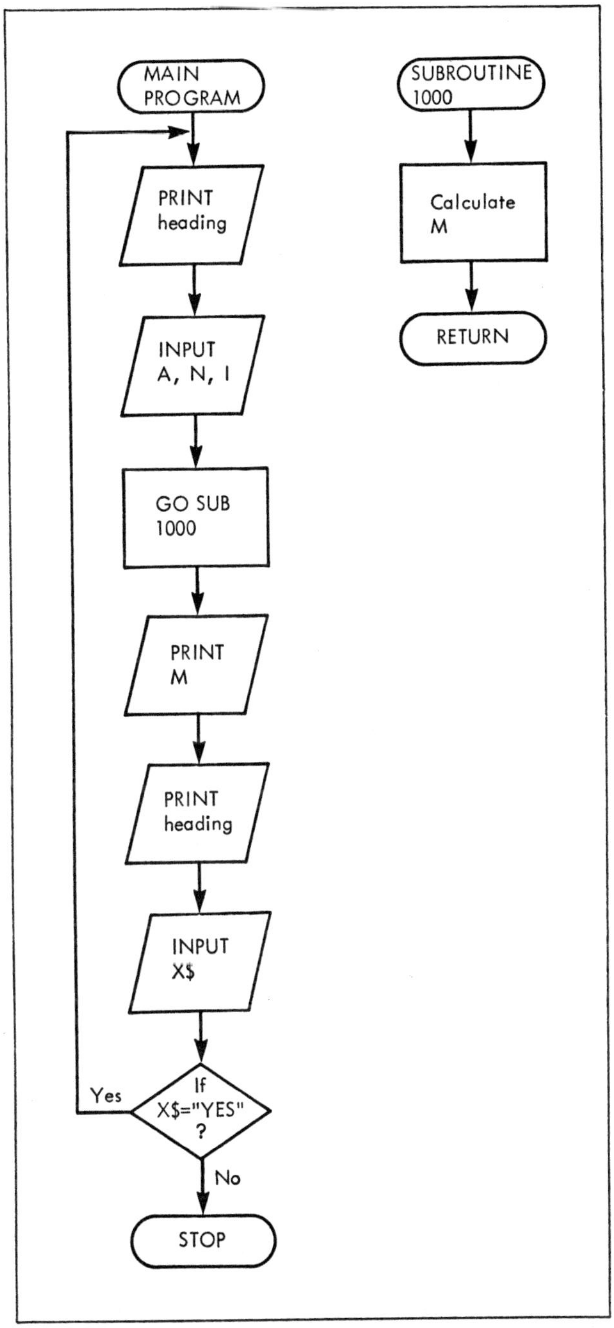

FIGURE 8-1
Flowchart for application 8-2

SUMMARY

Although any program can be written without the concepts discussed in this chapter, these concepts greatly simplify certain types of applications. When a complex expression or relationship is to be used, the DEF statement should be considered. In cases where several variables are to be used, a subroutine is in order. Of course, subroutines are very helpful when several programmers are working on a larger program.

QUESTIONS

8-1. Under what conditions would the DEF statement be useful in a BASIC program?

8-2. When would a subroutine be helpful in a BASIC program?

8-3. Which of the following DEF statements contain one or more errors:

a. 40 DEF X = 1 + X**2
b. 100 DEF FN(Z) = Z + 14
c. 14 DEF FNAB(K) = K + 1
d. 100 DEF FNP(P) = P**P
e. 14 DEF FAA(A) = A + 17
f. 20 DEF FNZ(X) = Z + 14
g. 40 DEF FNB(K) = K – 1 + K*2
h. 30 DEF FNA(Z) = Z**2 + 1
i. 25 DEF FNN(P) = SQR(P)
j. 31 DEF FNM(N) = 3(N + 1)

8-4. If 1010 RETURN were included in Program 8-2, what would be the result?

8-5. Modify Program 8-1 to compute interest at 6, 8, 10, 12, and 14 percent.

8-6. Write a program, using DEF, to compute the following expression, where X = 2, 3, and 4:

$$F(X) = \frac{1 + X^2}{X^2 - 1}$$

9 Matrix operations with MAT, READ, INPUT, PRINT, TRN, INV, IDN, and more

If you have succeeded in completing the previous chapters, you are doing well. It should be comforting to know that a knowledge of the concepts in this chapter is not essential. Indeed, everything that you will learn in this chapter can be done with FOR–NEXT loops and subscripted variables. Because you are reading these words, it can be concluded that either you or your instructor have decided that learning these techniques will be worthwhile. It is our intention to persuade you that the methods discussed in this chapter are valuable programming aids. If you occasionally process subscripted variables, this will not be a difficult task.

MAT STATEMENTS

Some of the computations that the computer performs for you using MAT statements are very complex. In fact, you could take an entire course in matrix operations and linear algebra at many colleges and universities. The approach taken in this chapter is to explain *what* each of the features accomplishes instead of *how* each feature works. Table 9-1 gives an overview of matrix operations on most computer systems.

To assist you in understanding the MAT statements in Table 9-1, several matrixes will be defined below and used throughout the chapter.

A(1, 1) = 1 A(1, 2) = 2 A(1, 3) = 1
A(2, 1) = 1 A(2, 2) = 1 A(2, 3) = 2
A(3, 1) = 2 A(3, 2) = 3 A(3, 3) = 4

TABLE 9-1
Overview of matrix operations

Statement	Explanation
20 MAT READ A,B	Reads two matrixes of numbers from DATA statements.
10 MAT INPUT C	Inputs one matrix called C from the terminal.*
30 MAT PRINT D	Prints a matrix.
50 MAT Z = A	Defines the matrix Z to be equal to the matrix A.
40 MAT X = B + C	Defines the matrix X to be equal to the sum of matrixes B and C.
100 MAT Y = X – Z	Defines the matrix Y to be equal to matrix X minus matrix Z.
300 MAT K = A*B	Defines the matrix K as equal to matrix A times matrix B.
250 MAT L = (K)*A	Defines matrix L as equal to the constant number K times matrix A.
210 MAT E = TRN(A)	Defines matrix E as the *transpose* of matrix A.
130 MAT G = INV(B)	Defines matrix G as the *inverse* of matrix B.
330 MAT F = IDN	Matrix F becomes an *identity* matrix.
420 MAT L = ZER	Matrix L is completely filled with zeroes.
550 MAT R = CON	Matrix R is completely filled with ones.

*On some computer systems, only a vector or list of numbers can be inputted with MAT INPUT.

These assignments can be presented in a more compact format as seen below:

$$A = \begin{pmatrix} 1 & 2 & 1 \\ 1 & 1 & 2 \\ 2 & 3 & 4 \end{pmatrix}.$$

Matrixes B and C are:

$$B = \begin{pmatrix} 1 & 4 & 3 \\ 1 & 1 & -1 \\ 2 & -2 & 0 \end{pmatrix}.$$

$$C = (0 \quad 3 \quad 1).$$

The convention used in identifying the elements or numbers in a matrix will be identical to the convention used in Chapter 6. Thus, each number in a matrix will be identified by its *row* number and its *column* number. B(2, 3), for example, is –1, the number in the *second row* and *third column* of matrix B. You may wish to review Chapter 6 if you do not understand this convention or procedure.

The general form of all matrix statements is

```
line # MAT [an action]
```

The *actions,* as seen in Table 9-1, are many and varied. *A matrix of numbers can be read, inputted, added, subtracted, multiplied, printed, and much more.* First, several elementary matrix operations will be explored, then more advanced techniques will be discussed. *Before any operations can be performed, the computer must know the size of the matrix, its number of rows and number of columns. This can be done in DIM statements at the beginning of the program or in MAT statements in the body of the program.*[1]

Application 9-1

In Application 6-7, two matrixes were read. Then the two matrixes were added, and the results were printed. Do you remember how many statements were used? There were almost 50 statements. Now, Program 9-1 accomplishes the same results for matrix A and matrix B.

Program 9-1

```
5 DIM C(3,3)
10 MAT READ A(3,3)
20 MAT READ B(3,3)
30 MAT C = A+B
40 MAT PRINT C
50 DATA 1,2,1,1,1,2,2,3,4
60 DATA 1,4,3,1,1,-1,2,-2,0
70 END

READY
RUNNH

 2          6          4

 2          2          1

 4          1          4
```

The flowchart graphically reveals the simplicity of the program (see Figure 9-1).

Do you see the advantage of MAT statements? It took only eight simple instructions to read, add, and print two matrixes. In Chapter 6, it took almost 50 statements with nested FOR-NEXT loops. The above program is shorter and easier to understand. Line 10 reads nine numbers into matrix A, and line 20 reads nine numbers into matrix B. Line 30 adds the two matrixes together, and line 40 prints the results. Line 50 contains the data for matrix A. As you would

[1] Some computer systems will not permit matrixes to be dimensioned in the body of the program in MAT statements.

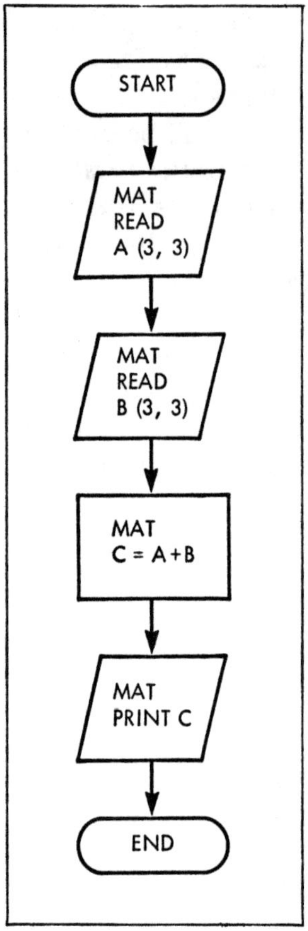

FIGURE 9-1
Flowchart for application 9-1

expect, the data is inserted in line 50 by rows for matrix A. The data for matrix B is in line 60.

The next application reveals several more MAT statements.

Application 9-2

B. K. Gerkin has been asked to input C. Then every number in C is to be multiplied by 3. This new matrix should be called D. Then C is to be subtracted from D to form another matrix called E. Matrixes D and E should be printed. See Program 9-2.

Program 9-2 makes the necessary computations. Observe the DIM statement in line 10. It tells the computer the size of the matrixes. Line 20 inputs C. Line 30 multiplies every number in C by 3, forming matrix D. In line 40, matrix E is set equal to matrix D minus matrix C. Then D and E are printed in lines 50 and 60. Look at the

Program 9-2

```
5 REM B. K. GERKIN
10 DIM C(3),D(3),E(3)
20 MAT INPUT C
30 MAT D = (3)*C
40 MAT E = D-C
50 MAT PRINT D
60 MAT PRINT E
70 END

READY
RUNNH

Matrix C ——→  ?0,3,1

               0
               9
Matrix D ——→   3

               0
               6
Matrix E ——→   2
```

output. (0, 9, 3) is 3 times C, which is (0, 3, 1). (0, 6, 2) is D − C or (0, 9, 3) − (0, 3, 1).

Here is another application. Two matrixes can be multiplied. The number of *columns* in the *first* matrix must be equal to the number of *rows* in the *second* matrix. Furthermore, the resulting matrix will have the same number of *rows* as the *first* matrix and the same number of *columns* as the *second* matrix. This seems very confusing until you see an example. Here is how you would multiply C by B by hand.

$$C \times B = (0 \quad 3 \quad 1) \times \begin{pmatrix} 1 & 4 & 3 \\ 1 & 1 & -1 \\ 2 & -2 & 0 \end{pmatrix}$$

$$= (0 \times 1 + 3 \times 1 + 1 \times 2,\ 0 \times 4 + 3 \times 1 + 1 \times (-2),$$
$$0 \times 3 + 3 \times (-1) + 1 \times 0)$$

$$= (5 \quad 1 \quad -3).$$

Do you see how the results are obtained? Matrix C has one row. Each element in this row was multiplied by the corresponding element in each column of B, and the products were added. For example, 5 ($5 = 0 \times 1 + 3 \times 1 + 1 \times 2$) is the row of C times the first column of B. In general each *row* in the *first* matrix is multiplied by each *column* in the *second* matrix. This fact is not too difficult to remember.

Larger matrixes are multiplied using the same approach. For example, *row 2* in the first matrix times *column 3* in the second matrix is the number in *row 2, column 3* of the new matrix, which shall be called E. Here is how this works for matrix A times matrix B.

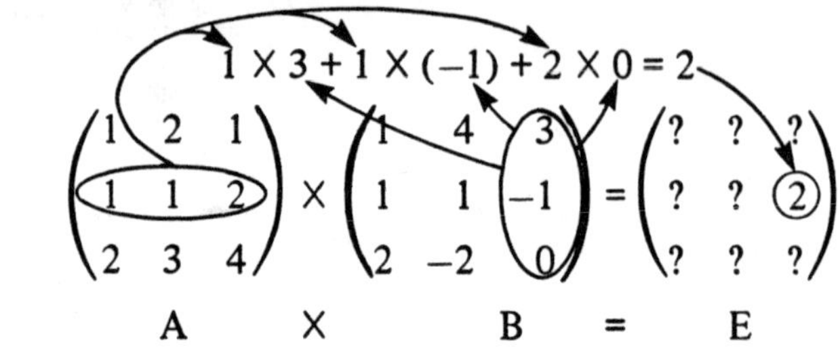

The same procedure is performed for every other row in the first matrix, A, and every other column in the second matrix, B. The results of (the new matrix E) appear below:

1×1+2×1+1×2 = ⑤;   1×4+2×1+1×(−2) = ④;   1×3+2×(−1)+1×0 = ①
1×1+1×1+2×2 = ⑥;   1×4+1×1+2×(−2) = ①;   1×3+1×(−1)+2×0 = ②
2×1+3×1+4×2 = ⑬;   2×4+3×1+4×(−2) = ③;   2×3+3×(−1)+4×0 = ③

Matrix multiplication can be long and tedious. It is refreshing to know that all of the computations can be made as a result of one statement:

```
MAT E = A*B
```

The following application confirms this feature.

Application 9-3

B. K. Gerkin has been asked to multiply A times C, and A times B. Program 9-3 accomplishes this objective.

Notice how the sizes of the matrixes are given in the READ statement in line 20 and in the DIM statement in line 5. Several matrixes can be read in one line. The same is true for PRINT statements as seen in line 50. 7, 5, and 13 are the numbers in matrix D. The 3 X 3 matrix that appears below matrix D, is matrix E. You may wish to multiply A*C and A*B to check your knowledge of matrix multiplication.

CON, ZER, IDN, TRN, AND INV

Some of the fundamental matrix operations have been explained, but there are also some special purpose functions that can be extremely helpful for certain problems. These special features are CON,

Program 9-3

```
5 DIM D(3,0),E(3,3)
10 REM B. K. GERKIN
20 MAT READ A(3,3,)B(3,3),C(3,0)
30 MAT D=A*C
40 MAT E= A*B
50 MAT PRINT D,E
60 DATA 1,2,1,1,1,2,2,3,4
70 DATA 1,4,3,1,1,-1,2,-2,0
80 DATA 0,3,1
90 END

READY
RUNNH

 7          5          13  <---------- Matrix D

 5          4          1

 6          1          2   <---------- Matrix E

 13         3          3
```

ZER, IDN, TRN, and INV. The following applications reveal the operation of these features.

Application 9-4

A. Shumway has been asked to define and print X, Y, and Z as the zero matrix, the constant one matrix, and the identity matrix. Then Shumway is to multiply A by the identity matrix. See Program 9-4.

The output from this program is self-explanatory. CON produces a matrix filled with ones; ZER produces a matrix filled with zeroes; and IDN produces a matrix with ones down the diagonal and zeroes

Program 9-4

```
10 REM A. SHUMWAY
20 DIM X(3,3),Y(3,3),Z(3,3),A(3,3),D(3,3)
30 MAT X = ZER
40 PRINT "THE ZER MATRIX IS BELOW"
50 MAT PRINT X
60 MAT Y = CON
70 PRINT "THE CON MATRIX IS BELOW"
80 MAT PRINT Y
90 MAT Z = IDN
100 PRINT "THE IDN MATRIX IS BELOW"
110 MAT PRINT Z
120 MAT READ A
130 DATA 1,2,1,1,1,2,2,3,4
140 MAT D = A*Z
150 PRINT "A TIMES IDN IS BELOW"
160 MAT PRINT D
170 END

READY
RUNNH
```

Output from Program 9-4

```
THE ZER MATRIX IS BELOW

0           0           0
0           0           0
0           0           0
THE CON MATRIX IS BELOW

1           1           1
1           1           1
1           1           1
THE IDN MATRIX IS BELOW

1           0           0
0           1           0
0           0           1
A TIMES IDN IS BELOW

1           2           1
1           1           2
2           3           4
```

elsewhere. It is important to note that IDN times A produces the matrix A. Furthermore, IDN times *any* matrix produces that matrix. IDN, the identity matrix, is a very important concept in matrix algebra. Two other important and commonly used concepts are the transpose and inverse of a matrix. Table 9-2 relates these concepts to BASIC.

The following application shows TRN and INV in action.

TABLE 9-2
Overview of transpose and inverse

Algebraic symbol*	*BASIC operator*	*Explanation*
X^1	TRN (X)	The transpose of X. The rows and columns are interchanged.
X^{-1}	INV (X)	The inverse of X. Note: $X \times X^{-1}$ is IDN, the identity matrix.

*Note: X is any matrix with the same number of rows and columns.

Application 9-5

M. Clay has been given an assignment to find the transpose and inverse of A. Then the inverse of A is to be multiplied by A. See Program 9-5.

Again, the Program 9-5 is straightforward. It calculates and prints A^1, which is TRN(A); A^{-1}, which is INV(A); and $A \times A^{-1}$, which is A times INV(A).

Program 9-5

```
10 REM M. CLAY
20 DIM A(3,3),I(3,3),T(3,3),R(3,3)
30 MAT READ A
40 DATA 1,2,1,1,1,2,2,3,4
50 MAT T = TRN (A)
60 PRINT "THE TRANSPOSE OF A IS BELOW"
70 MAT PRINT T
80 MAT I = INV (A)
90 PRINT "THE INVERSE OF A IS BELOW"
100 MAT PRINT I
110 MAT R = A*I
120 PRINT "A TIMES A INVERSE IS BELOW"
130 MAT PRINT R
140 END

READY
RUNNH


THE TRANSPOSE OF A IS BELOW

 1          1          2

 2          1          3

 1          2          4

THE INVERSE OF A IS BELOW

 2          5         -3

 0         -2          1

-1         -1          1

A TIMES A INVERSE IS BELOW

 1          0          0

 0          1          0

 0          0          1
```

SUMMARY

In this chapter, you have learned the fundamentals of matrix operations. Did you notice a lack of real applications in this chapter? Realistic and sophisticated applications were not included for a reason. Many students have difficulty digesting some of the complex matrix operations and sophisticated applications in one large gulp. Therefore, this chapter was designed to let you digest the main course, the fundamental matrix operations.

QUESTIONS

9-1. When would MAT statements be useful in a BASIC program?

9-2. Can MAT statements perform activities that could not be done otherwise?

9-3. Refer to line 10 in Program 9-1. How could you read matrix A without using a MAT statement?

9-4. Refer to line 30 in Program 9-1. How could you add matrix A and matrix B without a MAT statement?

9-5. Speaker Shop has two locations. One shop is in San Francisco, and the other is in Chicago. Last year, the San Francisco shop had the following sales in units:

Type of speaker	*Sales in units* 1st quarter	2d quarter	3d quarter	4th quarter
1	102	108	110	122
2	82	88	96	110
3	75	86	98	110
4	55	61	70	78
Super 4	85	96	107	115

The body of the table will be called matrix A.

$$A = \begin{pmatrix} 102 & 108 & 110 & 122 \\ 82 & 88 & 96 & 110 \\ 75 & 86 & 98 & 110 \\ 55 & 61 & 70 & 78 \\ 85 & 96 & 107 & 115 \end{pmatrix}$$

In a similar fashion, last year's sales in units for Chicago can be displayed in a matrix. Matrix B, below, contains the sales figures for Chicago.

$$B = \begin{pmatrix} 140 & 160 & 185 & 210 \\ 90 & 96 & 104 & 111 \\ 70 & 82 & 96 & 110 \\ 42 & 61 & 83 & 115 \\ 110 & 112 & 113 & 112 \end{pmatrix}$$

Write a program that reads and then prints matrix A and matrix B.

9-6. The president of Speaker Shop, Tom Murray, would like the total sales breakdown. Write a program that adds the two matrixes and then prints the results.

Data files with FILES, SCRATCH, RESTORE, READ, WRITE, and IF

10

Most organizations use permanent or master data files. An employee file, an inventory file, and a customer file are a few examples. These master files are normally kept on disk. So far, all the programs we have written READ data from DATA statements or INPUT data from a teletype or terminal. When thousands of data items are used in a program, a more efficient method of processing data is needed. How would you like to spend an entire day entering data with the teletype? You would most likely have to spend a second day checking to make sure that you did not make any mistakes. What a waste of time! Instead, it would be much more efficient to keep all important data on the disk. Then you could READ data directly from the disk and WRITE the results back onto the disk for future use.

CREATING DATA FILES

In most computer systems, you have two options in creating a data file. You can either create a data file as you would create any program, or write a program that writes data into a data file. First, we discuss how to create a data file like a program.

Application 10-1

The records of the first six employees in the employee master file are to be placed in a data file. For most computer systems, you use the same procedures to enter a file as you would to enter a program.

Illustration 10-1

```
NEW
NEW FILE NAME--EMFILE

READY

10 101,"SMITH R.","283-0114",4.80,1214.61
20 102,"ADAMS A.","481-2068",3.75,1001.10
30 103,"HOWE K.","283-3969",6.41,2013.23
40 104,"BREN D.","283-0444",3.10,1022.46
50 105,"BROWN B.","481-1424",5.85,1887.72
60 106,"DUDE K.","283-8914",4.45,1614.63

READY
```

Here is an example of how it can be done after you are in the BASIC mode on the terminal.[1]

Information that you insert has been underlined.

If your computer system does not permit you to create a file as shown above, a file can always be created by writing a program that writes the desired data to the file.

Application 10-2

The following computer program creates a file called IMFILE (Inventory Master File).[2]

Three new statements have been used in the program. Their general form appears below.

line # FILES [A list of file names separated by commas.]
line # SCRATCH # [A number from 0 through 9.]
line # WRITE # [A number from 0 through 9.], [A list of expressions]

Program 10-1

```
10 REM CREATE AN INVENTORY MASTER FILE
20 FILES IMFILE
30 SCRATCH #1
40 FOR I = 1 TO 7
50 READ P$,N$,P1,Q
60 WRITE #1,P$,N$,P1,Q
70 NEXT I
90 REM MASTER INVENTORY FILE
100 REM PART NO.,PART NAME, PRICE, QUANTITY
110 DATA "101","EX6",20.50,321
120 DATA "102","EX7",28.95,44
130 DATA "103","EX8",42.25,127
140 DATA "104","XX1",31.40,336
150 DATA "105","XX2",33.25,556
160 DATA "106","XX5",41.50,133
170 DATA "107","XXY",108.90,56
9000 END
```

[1] For some computer systems, this procedure may be slightly different. For other computer systems, this procedure may not be allowed.

[2] Some computers may not need the FILES or SCRATCH commands. Some computers may use a different WRITE statement, such as WRITE: IMFILE: P$, N$, P1, Q.

You may have to save the file for future use. It all depends on your computer system. If you have to save the file IMFILE, here is how it is done on most computer systems:

```
SAVE IMFILE
```

The FILES statement tells the computer that data files are to be used. A file name must start with a letter, consist of letters and numbers only, and be six or fewer characters. The first file in the FILES statement will be referred to as #1 in the rest of the program, the second file will be #2, the third file will be #3, and so on. For example #1 in the SCRATCH and WRITE statements refers to the first (and only) file in the FILES statement. This file is IMFILE. *The SCRATCH command is needed before information is to be written in a file.* SCRATCH #1 makes the first file in the FILES statement, IMFILE, ready to accept data from the program. *WRITE #1 is just like the PRINT statement, but it writes in the first file in the FILES statement. WRITE #2 would write in the second file, and so forth.*

When a company or other organization decides to computerize, all their manual files must be placed in computerized data files as discussed above. This is a time-consuming and expensive task, but it has to be done only once. Then these files can be maintained and used efficiently to produce meaningful output.

THE USE OF DATA FILES

One type of report that is very useful to managers is the *demand report.* This type of report is produced only when it is needed by a manager: it is produced on demand.

Application 10-3

It is 5:30 p.m. It has been a very busy week, and because it is Friday, almost everyone is gone for the weekend except for Jim Blake, the sales manager. The phone rings. It is the new sales representative, calling long-distance. She is just about to close a deal for 500 units of a product called XX2. Her client needs all 500 units. Is there enough XX2 on hand to fill the order?

Fortunately Jim wrote a program that will print the complete inventory record for any item in inventory. The program is shown in Program 10-2.

Two new statements were used in Program 10-2. Their general form appears below:

```
line # RESTORE # [a number from 0 through 9]
line # READ # [a number from 0 through 9]  [a list of variables]
```

Program 10-2

```
5 FILES IMFILE
10 RESTORE #1
20 PRINT "DEMAND REPORT FOR MR. J. BLAKE."
30 PRINT
40 PRINT "ENTER ITEM NAME"
50 INPUT N$
60 PRINT
70 PRINT "NUMBER","NAME","PRICE","QUANTITY"
80 FOR I = 1 TO 7
90 READ #1,M,M$,P,Q
100 IF M$<>N$, THEN 120
110 PRINT M,M$,P,Q
115 GO TO 130
120 NEXT I
130 END

READY
RUNNH


DEMAND REPORT FOR MR. J. BLAKE.

ENTER ITEM NAME
 ?XX2

NUMBER          NAME            PRICE           QUANTITY
 105            XX2              33.25           556
```

RESTORE #1 in line 10 prepares IMFILE for reading. Some computer systems do not require the RESTORE *statement. READ #1, M, M$, P, Q is identical to the READ statement except the data is read from the first file in the FILES statement–IMFILE.*

In line 50, the name of the inventory item is inputted. A FOR–NEXT loop starts in line 80. Line 90 reads inventory records one at a time, and line 100 determines whether the inventory names match. If they are the same, the computer prints the record for the item in line 110. Otherwise, the computer continues to search the data for the desired inventory item.

The above program is short and convenient; it contains no DATA statements. Although the data file contains only six records, this program would work if there were thousands of inventory items.

Application 10-4

Two years ago, a high-priced consultant recommended that inventory levels be reduced. He claimed that the company had too much money invested in inventory. Unfortunately, the company adopted the consultant's recommendation. As a result of lower inventory levels, there were many stockouts, and several important customers went to other companies. To avoid losing any more customers, the vice president of marketing insisted that an exception report be prepared by the computer. This report would contain a list of all inventory items with 100 or fewer units on hand. An order would be immediately placed for any item on this list. The program is shown in Program 10-3.

A new statement has been used. It has the following form.[3]

line # IF END # [a number from 0 through 9] [THEN or GO TO] line #

Program 10-3

```
10 FILES IMFILE
20 RESTORE #1
30 PRINT "EXCEPTION REPORT"
35 PRINT
40 PRINT "AN ORDER FOR THE FOLLOWING ITEMS";
50 PRINT " SHOULD BE PLACED IMMEDIATELY."
60 PRINT
70 PRINT "PART NO.","NAME,","PRICE","QUANTITY"
80 READ #1,P$,N$,P1,Q
90 IF Q > 100, THEN 110
100 PRINT P$,N$,P1,Q
110 IF END #1, THEN 130
120 GO TO 80
130 END

READY
RUNNH


EXCEPTION REPORT

AN ORDER FOR THE FOLLOWING ITEMS SHOULD BE PLACED IMMEDIATELY.

PART NO.      NAME         PRICE        QUANTITY
102           EX7           28.95        44
107           XXY           108.9        56
```

The above statement is like any other IF statement. If the end of the file is encountered, the computer goes to the indicated line number. In Program 10-3 the computer is directed to go to line 130. Otherwise, the computer drops down to the next statement and continues as usual.

SUMMARY

This chapter has been devoted to the creation and use of data files. Two ways of creating data files were developed, and several different uses of data files were investigated.

Congratulations! You have successfully completed a course in BASIC programming. The road was not always smooth or easy, but this journey will pay off. As a student and as a professional in a work environment, you will find a knowledge of computers and programming to be essential.

[3] Some computer systems do not allow the IF END statement.

QUESTIONS

10-1. Use the following data to create a data file called A. Then write a short program to list the file.

Data file A (employee master file)

No.	*Name*	*Phone*	*Pay rate*	*Earnings to date*	*Classi-fication*
100	LEBOEUF, M.	233-6104	6.70	1100	W1
110	VILLERE, M.	233-0488	6.70	890	W1
130	STILLMAN, D.	233-1112	7.10	890	W2
150	JUHN, D.	899-1106	5.90	1120	C1
160	CHARLTON, J.	233-1301	4.80	841	W2
180	HALL, O.	233-1122	6.20	862	C2
190	RENDER, B.	899-8111	6.62	814	W1
200	CROMARTIE, J. . . .	899-1462	6.36	837	C3
220	ROBBINS, S.	899-8989	4.36	798	W3
240	PETTINGILL, B. . .	233-3131	5.27	867	W1
250	O'CONNOR, T.	233-6931	7.28	1221	C2
260	REINECKE, J.	233-4142	6.60	1010	C1
270	STEARNS, K.	899-1661	5.39	998	W1
280	LUNDBERG, O.	899-1432	4.20	891	W3

10-2. Use the following data to create a data file called B. Then write a short program to list the file.

Data file B (inventory master file)

No.	*Name*	*Price*	*Quantity*	*Reorder point*
200	EXT 1	67.40	320	50
210	EXT 4	32.70	1260	50
230	EXT 6	41.40	46	50
260	EXT 4	89.95	1071	100
300	MOD 3	126.00	221	50
310	MOD 6	42.30	364	200
340	MOD 9	55.40	400	200
360	SYS 1	62.60	1000	200
410	SYS 7	41.41	41	100

10-3. Use the following data to create a data file called C. Then write a short program to list the file.

Data file C (inventory master file)

No.	*Name*	*City*	*State*	*Credit*
10	MLPFS	NEW ORLEANS	LA	AAA
20	CANCO	NEW ORLEANS	LA	A
40	IDS	SAN FRANCISCO	CA	AA
80	PMM	SAN DIEGO	CA	AAA
85	AA	LODI	FL	AA
90	EE	TALLAHASSEE	FL	AAA
100	PWIC	BOSTON	MA	A

10-4. Write a program to calculate the average pay rate and total earnings to date for all employees in data file A.

10-5. Whenever the quantity of an item falls below the reorder point, an order should be placed for that particular item. Write a program to list the entire record for all such inventory items in data file B.

Index

A

ANSI template for application and program flowcharting, 4
Application flowchart, 5-7
  card file, 4
  computer program (process), 4
  direct access file, 4
  display, 4
  document, 4
  and symbol of usage, 3
Arithmetic expression, 22
  conversion to BASIC, 25
  evaluation of, 24
Arithmetic operators, 23-24

B

BASIC features, 90
  PRINT USING, 81-84
  random numbers, 87-89
  string variables and constants, 79-81
  TAB, 84-87
BASIC fundamental concepts, 27
  E notation, 21-22
  expressions, 23-25
  numbers, 21
  predefined functions, 22-23
  REM statement (remarks), 25-26
  statements and line numbers, 22
  variables, 22
BASIC program and application development
  computer system analysis, 3-7
  computer system requirements, 2-3
  for creating loops that cycles once for each value in the data statement, 115
  as a hand calculation, 13
  for instructing the computer before results are printed, 14
  postprogramming activities, 8-10
  preprogramming activities (planning), 1-2
  programming, 8
BASIC programmer, 10-11
BASIC programming, 78
  DIMENSION statements, 70-77
  FOR and NEXT statements, 59
  RESTORE statements, 68-69
  subscripted variables, 69-70
BASIC realistic programs, 57
  GO TO, 49-52
  IF, 52-54
  INPUT, 47-49
  ON–GO TO, 54-56
  READ and DATA statements, 45-47
BASIC simple programs, 43
  END, 29
  LET, 34-39
  PRINT, 29-34
  undefined variables (possible errors), 39-42
BASIC subroutines and user-defined functions, 46
  DEF, 91-93
  GO SUB–RETURN, 93-95
Bugs (programming mistakes), 8-10

C

Card file, 4
Computer cards, 3
Computer program (process), 4, 11
Computer program analysis
  application flowchart, 3-7
  exception report program, 2-4, 6, 9
  for processing input data, 3
Computer program requirements
  input, 2-3
  output, 2-3
Computer system analysis, 3-7

D

Data files, 112-13
  creating data files, 107-9
  demand report, 109

Data files–*Cont.*
files, 109
IF, 110-11
IMFILE, 108
master files, 107
READ, 107
RESTORE, 110
SCRATCH, 109
use of data file, 109-11
WRITE, 107, 109
Data processing department, 2-3
Data processing manager, 2-3
DATA statement, 15, 45-47
Data storage
computer card, 3
disk, 3
tape, 3
DEF, 91-93
"dummy" variable, 89
Demand report, 109
DIM statement, 79, 99
DIMENSION statement, 70-77
Direct access file, 4
Document, 4

E

E notation, 21-22
END statement
"no more statements in the program," 29
terminating program execution, 29
Exception report program, 2, 4-6, 9, 54
Expression, 21, 23

F

Field (PRINT), message or expression (up to 15 spaces), 33
FILES statement, 109
Flowchart, 5, 7, 14, 30-31, 36-37, 46, 50, 61, 65-66, 73, 95, 99-100; *see also* Application flowchart *and* Program flowchart
as specification for computer program, 3
FOR–NEXT loops, 65, 67, 71-72, 76-77, 110
FOR statement, 60-67

G

GO SUB, 93-95
GO TO, 26, 49, 52
loop, 50-51
Grammatical error, 9, 17

H

Hierarchy of operations, 24
Hierarchy of operators, 24

I

IF, 52
branching, 56
exception reports, 56
loops, 56
IMFILE (inventory master file), 108-10
Implementation
parallel reporting, 10
phase in, 10
phase out of manual report, 10
INPUT, 47-49
Input data from teletype or terminal, 107
Input data storage
computer cards, 3
disk, 3
tape, 3
Input requirements, 2, 11
data statements, 3
variables, 3

K

Keyword, for instructing the computer to perform task, 26

L

LET statement, 26, 35-39
a definition that assigns a value or number to a variable, 34
information storage, 34
line number, 26
Logical error, 17, 69
Loops
FOR, 59, 67, 110
FOR–NEXT, 59, 65, 67, 71-72, 76-77, 81, 110
GO TO, 50-51

M

Main storage (memory), 69-70, 76
Master file, 5, 107
MAT statement, 97, 99-102
Matrix operations, 98, 100, 106
CON, ZER, IDN, TRN, and INV, 102-5
DIM statement, 99
INPUT, 99
MAT, 97
PRINT, 99
READ, 99

N

NEXT statement, 26, 60-67
and loop, 59
Numbers, 21, 23

O

ON–GO TO
branching and alternative paths, 54
computer aided instruction (CAI), 55-56
Operator, 23
Out-of-data error message, 15, 40, 50, 66
Output
document, 4
report, 2-3, 5
Output requirements, 2-3

P

Postprogramming
  implementation, 10
  testing, 8-11
Predefined functions, 21-23
Preprogramming activities (planning), 1
  analysis, 3-7
  requirements, 2-3
PRINT, 26
  comma, 29-31
  field (up to 15 spaces), 33
  semicolon, 29-31
  special format options, 33
PRINT statement features
  comma sets up normal spacing between fields, 33
  message in quotation marks, 33
  prints blank message where called for, 33
  at statement end, space left empty, moves to next line, 33
PRINT USING, 81-84
Processing input data, 3
Program flowchart, 11
  FOR–NEXT (loops), 6
  IF (all decisions), 6
  LET (all processing), 6
  READ and PRINT (all input and output), 6
  START and END, 6
  and symbol use, 5, 7-8
Program instruction, 7
Program statement, 10
Programmer, 8
  BASIC programmer commands computer, 16
Programming and program flowchart, 8
Programming mistakes (bugs), 8-10

R

Random numbers
  random sample, 88
  RND function, 87-89
  and simulating random events, 89
RANDOMIZE, 87
READ data from DATA statement, 107
READ statements, 45-48
REM statement (remarks), 25
  and program purpose, 26
Report, exception, 2-6, 9
RESTORE, 68-69, 110
RND function, 87-89

S

Statement number, 21
STOP statement, 94
Storage area (memory), 37-39, 52
String constants, 79-80
String variables, 80
  DIM, 79
  IF, 79
  INPUT, 79
  LET, 79
  PRINT, 79
  READ, 79
Subroutine
  GO SUB–RETURN, 93-95
  STOP statement, 94
Subscripted variables, 69-70
  computer memory analyzing matrixes, 74-75

T

TAB, 84-87
Tape storage, 3
Template, 3-4, 6
Testing, 11
  for programming mistakes (bugs), 8-10
  of statements, 9-10

U-W

Undefined variable (a possible error source), 39-42
Variables, 21-23
Writing BASIC programs, 16-19

This book has been set IBM in 11 and 10 point Press Roman. Chapter titles are 18 point Oracle Bold. The size of the text area is 27 by 48 picas.